The Ultimate Camp
Counselor Manual

The Ultimate Camp Counselor Manual

✦

(How To Survive And Succeed Magnificently At Summer Camp)

Second Edition

Mark S. Richman

Author of the best-seller: Just Let Me Survive Today!

iUniverse, Inc.

New York Lincoln Shanghai

The Ultimate Camp Counselor Manual
(How To Survive And Succeed Magnificently At Summer Camp)

iUniverse books may be ordered through booksellers or by contacting:

iUniverse
2021 Pine Lake Road, Suite 100
Lincoln, NE 68512
www.iuniverse.com
1-800-Authors (1-800-288-4677)

ISBN-13: 978-0-595-40832-0 (pbk)
ISBN-13: 978-0-595-85194-2 (ebk)
ISBN-10: 0-595-40832-X (pbk)
ISBN-10: 0-595-85194-0 (ebk)

Printed in the United States of America

DEDICATION

I would like to dedicate this book to Mr. Joe Laub, the founder of Trail's End Camp, from whom I learned all about Values Education, and who inspired me to become a successful educator and parent. I would also like to dedicate the book to the current owner of Trail's End Camp"—Mr. Stan Goldberg. When I was at Trail's End, Stan was Boy's Head Counselor. He was a wonderfully sensitive leader who taught me so many things about kind, considerate, human relations—oriented leadership, along with more superb ideas for values education. I have carried Stan and Joe's teachings with me into my career as a teacher, administrator, and parent.

I also dedicate this book to my beautiful and wonderful daughter Rachel, and to my equally beautiful and wonderful wife Sharon, both of whom have shown me the wonders of parenthood and marriage, respectively.

As an amazing bonus, as I explain in partial detail in Chapter One, Rachel has shown me the enormous resilience of camping itself. Through her amazing summer experiences, she has brought back (and even enhanced for me) the wonders of summer camp. The experience seems to have gotten even better!! Rachel, may you (and millions of other kids) continue to feel the amazing "good" of the summer camp experience.

Contents

1

Who Am I?

I began my long journey at Trails End Camp in July of 1959. It was (and still is as of this writing) a wonderful co-ed camp in the Pocono Mountains in a little town named Beach Lake, Pa. The founder and director of this camp was named Joseph Laub and he founded the camp in around 1946. The "motto" of Trail's End was "Truth, Ethics and Courage." Mr. Laub had an idealistic vision of life and the way things "ought to be." He was fair, a great leader, and at every turn tried to educate all members of the TEC (Trail's End Camp) community with his lofty ideals. It truly was a wonderful place, where, if one could become "plugged into" his wavelength, one could really grow as a person—and become, as his other slogan went, "better for having been" at TEC.

So on this fine, bright, sunny day in the summer of '59, off I went, as a scared little nine year old, for the first time away from his home, crying on the bus as I saw the image of my mother and father fade into teary-eyed obscurity on Ave L and Bedford Avenue in Brooklyn, just a stone's throw away from the home of Brooklyn Dodger hero Gil Hodges. Separation anxiety to the 10th power (I'm a math teacher today) is what I suffered from—and continued to suffer from for a long while up there. In any event, I spent the next 6 summers as a camper. I followed that up with 2 as a waiter and then 17 years as a counselor. I believe that hardly anyone on this earth has spent 25 summers at one summer camp. These experiences give me the unique opportunity to write this book and pass on all of the insights gathered from these experiences to you folks.

Linked in with all of this is the fact that since 1973, I have been an award-winning, successful teacher with the NY Public School System—partly as a direct result of my camping background.

I had the fortunate chance to experience camp from all of the perspectives mentioned above—camper, waiter and staff member. In addition, I spent 8 of my counseling years as a general counselor, then four as a "unit-head" or group-leader. I followed this up with 5 as an assistant athletic director. Throughout the period I worked with children of all ages. In addition, during my counseling years, I often served as "M.C." for the evening programs, and I often was referred to as "Director of Mishigos," the latter word meaning good natured "craziness" in Yiddish. These years in camping provided me with those rich experiences which I would now like to pass onto you—the novice counselor, or perhaps even to the veteran seeking to improve his or her skills.

As mentioned, greatly attributable to my experiences in camping is the fact that I have been a successful 33 year veteran teacher. Many of my teaching skills are the direct result of camp life. Let me briefly summarize my career in education. Please at this time turn to Appendix Figure 16 for this summary, which is an excerpt from my book "Just Let Me Survive Today."

So you see, my successful experience with children has been of over 33 year duration, is all year long, and has spanned many age levels. All of this experience and success, coupled with my introspective, caring, kind personality and great sensitivity, has given me the extra-special qualifications to write this book. I've been in the "trenches." I'm still there! And I still love it after all these years.

Education and camping are great fields of endeavor. There is much opportunity for creativity and for positively affecting the future lives of our children and hence our planet. It is extremely rare to find a field where so much good can be accomplished for oneself and for others. Have a super career—but first a super summer!

Here in fall of 2006, my daughter has just returned from her second full summer of "sleep away" camp—Camp Ramah in the Berkshires. It was simply an amazingly wonderful and magical experience for her. Her letters home were happy, cheerful, and upbeat. She looked wonderful. She had friends hanging off her like "groupies" off a rock star.

In my talking to her about camp, memories of my 25 year journey were rekindled. Many of the same reasons I loved camp still ring true today—almost 30-40 years later. In fact, it seems even better.

She tells me stories of counselors singing nightly to the kids as they enter "sleep mode." In fact, there seemed to be one counselor who sang the same hauntingly beautiful song (with her amazing superstar voice) to Rachel's bunk every single night and then gave all the kids a CD of many of the camp favorites—including that one song.

There are tales of a bunk working as a team. I ask about discipline—discipline with dignity, etc. It seems that there was no need for disciplinary intervention…the kids are that good.

Rachel had a nickname at camp—"Jelly"—owing to her love for peanut butter and jelly. Well, "my counselor loved me so much that she called me "Jelly—Love." There are similar tales of warmth and kindness that describe Rachel's counselors at Ramah.

There are the 100 or so photos a day that are posted for parents to view on the camp website, as well as opportunities to send daily E-mails using the technology of the year 2006.

But mostly there are those same wonderfully sensitive qualities exhibited by a caring staff that made my camp experience so wonderful back in 1959. These feelings remain constant—in fact in this case of Rachel—even get better.

Counselors at Ramah seemed to have built a wonderful community where rules are obeyed because of mutual respect, caring and love. Some things never seem to change—except to get even better!!

2

The Web

We begin here by discussing The Web. It will provide the basis for dealing with problems, for planning activities and for just about everything else during the summer. There is a picture illustrating this Web in the Appendix at Figure One. In the center is "Successful Problem Solving" of all kinds. For nearly every situation that we must deal with, I may refer you to The Web and illustrate how its unique power can be tapped. Every problem can be made that much easier to solve by referring to This Web Of Solutions. Let's here discuss each component aspect of it in general and then refer to it, as needed, throughout the rest of the book.

Start with those "One On One Discussions." You sit down with the camper and just talk face to face. You say what is on your mind. It might be advisable to jot down a few notes on what you want to say. Your talk should have a purpose and a method. Again, organize your thoughts on paper before you begin your one on one. As your talk proceeds, play it by ear as to how to continue. Always keep in mind the sensitivities of your camper. The more you know about the child and the better the relationship you have established with him, the better will be the results of your one on one talk with him. Of course the methodology will differ for each particular age group and each situation but the purpose and goal remain consistent. Always go with one on ones as often as possible. I even did this effectively with my 2 1/2 year old daughter (who is now 12). It "sinks in" on some level. It is a first step. I've used this one on one technique for 33 years as a teacher and it is a featured highlight of my first book—"Just Let Me Survive Today." It does work! Use it!

Then comes the "Group Discussion." By this I mean the previously mentioned group guidance (good and welfare) situation. These include the evening sessions in the bunk, rest hour talks or talks at just any time which take place as a group. In all these, the opportunity you get is to explain rules, philosophies, and debate and discuss critical or "hot" issues, etc. There is usually a chance for lots of give and take at this time. It is another component in The Web that leads to improved behavior patterns, attitudes and values. Continuing. Every moment ("Minute By Minute Seize The Opportunity") provides you with a chance to teach: when you're on the ball fields, in the dining room, walking to activity, at campfires, etc. These moments will also increase the bonds of trust that are slowly being formed between all involved—a bond that you can tap into later as needed for the extra energy and power that might be essential to solving a tough problem. Also, these informal teaching moments will help to break down any barriers that may be necessary to dismantle in the healthy psychological adjustment of the camper with problems (and everyone of course has some).

The next big component of The Web comes through Values Education. My book, "High Caliber Kids" is a lesson by lesson guide on the topic. It teaches values mainly through sports. Let me give a small excerpt from the flyer advertising this book: (Appendix Figure 5). The camp setting can provide an excellent venue for the implementation of many of these lessons. They may take the form of lectures, role playing activities, trips, plays or much more. The purpose is to increase the awareness in your campers of high-caliber values and to strive to use this awareness to help them become better camp citizens and hence more well adjusted individuals.

It is always a great idea to enlist the support of "Role Models" to try and serve as an example to the kids of desired behavior and/or attitudes. Famous athletes and show biz personalities—if available, can usually be extremely effective. Even high-caliber members of the adult camp community can serve as excellent teaching resources to the impressionable camper. Remember, every little step gets us closer to completion of our journey of a thousand miles. And for every inch we move along the path—we are much better off as human beings. We are making progress! We will get there!

Moving further along around The Web: "Enforceable, Reasonable Rules" are an essential framework for the campers to have. The structure that rules provide cannot be underestimated. With rules come enforcement techniques, for without the latter, the rules become meaningless. We cover this whole topic in Chapter 3. However, I mention it here because it will again help our problem-solving techniques enormously to have them in place. The campers will feel an added sense of security by the fact that there are folks that care enough about them to have established a complete set of enforceable rules. Another brick in the wall of trust between camper and counselor!

"Quality Time." Another very big component of The Web. The counselor must spend time with his campers. He (the counselor) must talk to the camper,

Empathy

listen to him, be sensitive to his needs of the moment, laugh with him, cry with him, feel his pain, feel his joy. Only by spending this intense quality time will he earn the respect that will be very necessary in order to help solve the tough problems that will arise.

There is "The Media": Movies, videos, songs, TV shows, plays, puppet shows, more. These and many other "show-bizzy" items can provide a wealth of learning opportunities in a wonderful framework of fun, spurred on by the charismatic attractiveness of some of the most creative minds in the world of children's and young adult's quality entertainment. These presentations can be arranged for evening activities, on rainy days, at free play time, rest hour, etc. They provide another technique of problem solving through education. After viewing the various pieces, various follow-up activities can be implemented—ranging from role play to discussion to brainstorming to just plain enjoying. Also, campers can be called on to create their own media "shows"—songs, newspaper articles, plays, videos, etc. Yet another source for learning and problem solving! See Appendix Figure 6 for an excerpt from my book "High Caliber Kids" on a combination of Media and Values Education.

The next component of The Web is the often referred to Chapter 4. This is the chapter that advises you on solving some of those "knothole" problems that seem like they'll just never get solved. It gives you hope that there are solutions out there so just don't ever give up—on your kids or yourself!

Also we see that successful results as a camp counselor do require The Web components of "Patience, Perseverance and Experience." These necessary qualities will be touched upon in various parts of this book. Just remember to keep asking questions, keep striving to improve, keep "Networking" (another Web component) with colleagues and supervisors, read camp literature and know that if you want to, each day, as you gain more and more experience in your job, you will become better and better as a counselor, an advisor and a friend to your campers and colleagues. Remember you're working with kids—doing some extremely important work! You have the opportunity of shaping the future through our children, a golden opportunity that virtually no other profession or job offers. Make the most of it! Use the components of the Web to your advantage.

Just what is "Shtick And Mishigos?" Well, I believe that I described it well in my book "Just Let Me Survive Today." Thus, I now enclose an excerpt from that book to clarify my definition:

Every class has rules that must be followed, work that must be covered, tests that must be administered. However, there has to be a time for fun. I am a teacher who always injects a bit of "mishigos" (Yiddish for "craziness") into the class day. At times, this takes the form of a math game. Other times, I try to use humor at the appropriate moment. The pupils love the change of pace and they get to see that their teacher has a human side, a fun side. My relationship with them is greatly enhanced because of this approach. Other than games, riddles and jokes, I often have certain "crazy" days or unique "show biz" events. It is these "show biz" happenings or routines that I refer to as the Yiddish word "shtick." "Shtick" is Abbot and Costello doing "Who's On First" and "Niagara Falls." It is Jack Benny, when asked, "Your money or your life?" saying: "Let me think it over!" It is what "Just Let Me Survive Today" is partially about and is the purpose of this chapter.

In it will be discussed some of the wild things that are done in class. Of course not all of you will feel comfortable doing some of what I discuss here. It is meant for your consideration. Keep an open mind. Pick and choose! Do what you think might work for you. You and your pupils will love these unique events and happenings. They'll often comment: "This teacher is nuts." But you will feel the emotional bonds in your room strengthen.

First we must have a very important discussion about this chapter and correspondingly about every other chapter in this book. The ideas contained in this book have been developed gradually over my long career. They do not just "happen" in the classroom on their own. Every single "event" takes planning, creating and refining. Let me explain: Take "Elvis Day." The idea for this day, or any other "happening," comes to me from any and every source—my own ideas, a student suggestion, a TV show, etc. I then start thinking about it and how I might adapt it to my classroom teaching. Perhaps it is a TV game show that I saw. I think some more and begin writing down my ideas. I set up an almost exact minute by minute accounting of specifically how and when in the period I will proceed in class with the "event." It is similar to writing a lesson plan, or even a play. All contingencies must be considered. I start getting very excited about my game plan and its implementation.

I am at "the try it out on my best class" time of idea development. I stage it for them. Again it is fully planned out as to time and sequence and as to how I want it to develop. It works well—or perhaps miserably. I go back to the "drawing board" and refine the ideas some more. I try it out again…and again. I vary its timing, introduction, etc. It usually gets better and better each time. Finally it becomes an established piece of "shtick" or "mishigos" and it takes its place as part of my repertoire.

Be a scientist → experiment, observe

I have always been a "show-biz" guy and each performance for me is like another Broadway presentation before a new audience. Before "opening night" you may need to do your minute by minute rehearsal in front of a mirror or friends. Never fear failure! No matter what, you and your class will have fun. So remember this discussion as you read about the many events throughout the book! None of these activities just "happen" out of nowhere on their own. Every single one goes through a similar birth and development process. Some of this "growing-up" occurs rapidly and some quite slowly. Every "happening" is "born" in its own unique way, and is creatively raised and nurtured until it becomes ready for its "coming out." So, after lots of hard work and creativity, opening night finally takes place. With multiple refinements every one of these events eventually becomes part of the aforementioned Richman repertoire. Now, "let the games begin."

What about "Safety?" Of course you do not want to get too overprotective, but for each area, you (and the activity specialist and camp administration) must have safety guidelines established and be ever vigilant. One severe injury can ruin the summer for everyone. The kids can still enjoy the activity, but never forget that you are entrusted with the lives and safety of your kids. This is obviously a huge and important responsibility. Rise to the occasion! Your future parenting skills are also being honed in your role as counselor.

"Brainstorming" is simply sitting down (often with collaborators) and coming up with as many ideas on a given topic as is possible—using "Your Own Creative Ideas" as well as those of colleagues, administrators, campers and just about anyone and everyone else who may be helpful.

"Your Philosophy" must be inherent in all of your planning and implementation. It is the heart and soul of your work. Let me present my philosophy of education, as excerpted from my "Survive" book:

Any program must begin with a basic philosophy. Of course, the learning of the actual subject matter is of great importance. However, those often-neglected affective aspects of education are to me critical, and of utmost urgency. They are a big priority. I wrote a "Sports Curriculum" a few years ago to help teach values through sports. In the introduction, I wrote:

> "Our planet has at times been on the brink of nuclear disaster. The subject matter of values, getting along with others and all other aspects of trait and character development are of extreme timeliness. If this subject matter is not employed today, we may not reach tomorrow. Through sports, we can teach the appreciation of basic values, as well as the responsibilities we all have as members of society."

Herein lies the key to my educational philosophy. We must teach students how to get along with and respect one another. We must help to build their self-confidence and self-esteem. We must teach them how to socialize. Every aspect of good human relations must be illustrated to our pupils. We want them to enjoy learning, perhaps even to love their subjects, and to have fun in school. We need for our children to learn how to communicate more effectively and to be able to express themselves in their lives. Finally come the cognitive aspects of skill development.

In applying to become a school administrator in New York City, I was required to fill out an application over eight pages long. One question was to explain my philosophy of education. I will reprint it here, because it further summarizes much of what I want you to know about me:

"I have worked as a counselor for fifteen years in a summer camp run by a director with a truly idealistic vision of society "the way it ought to be." This, in combination with my own substantial professional and personal growth, has served to inject in me a spirit and optimism that almost anything is possible—a feeling which I hope to convey to all of those with whom I come in contact.

In my life experiences I have found that certain traits are very important. Among them are kindness, consideration for the rights and property of others, politeness, responsibility, dependability, loyalty and integrity. I believe the children are our future and we are entrusted with most important work. By using our knowledge, experience and insight, we must help all of those we touch become better for having known us. We must teach, however, that change requires time, patience and hard work. We must stress honesty and not allow for manipulative behavior.

We must experiment and investigate to discover the needs of our students. Once accomplished, we must vary our instructional strategies and the nature of our relationships with our students depending on the unique situation at hand. We must set up our schools so that all involved have high probability of having frequent "peak" experiences. Only when pupils are very interested in and excited about the subject matter, either for practical or spiritual reasons, can we expect them to experience these wonderful feelings.

I am seeking this position because I feel that my philosophy, as just explained, combined with my vast educational experience, optimism, great enthusiasm and love for children, will all combine to result in a highly positive and effective outcome for all involved.

All the various components of my program are permeated by the spirit living within my educational philosophy."

3

Rules For Everything That Could Ever Happen

One of The Web components is "Enforceable, Reasonable, Rules." Rules are extremely important—they are truly the backbone of camp life. Without them there is chaos, confusion and possibly danger and injury. How does one compose the rules? Sit down before camp begins, brainstorm, and write down a list of what to you are your most important rules. If you've been counseling before, you'll know which ones to include. If you're a rookie, then ask colleagues and supervisors for suggestions. You can adapt and change your rules as needed—they are your creation! Your rules should be thoughtful, creative, reasonable, necessary, and enforceable. Do not make rules which you have no chance to enforce. They will be "elastic" in that they can be amended during the summer. They must fit your own unique style and personality. In my first book, "Just Let Me Survive Today," I have 2 chapters on rules for the classroom. The idea behind them is the same as that for this chapter. I will present (in the Appendix Figure 2) some appropriate excerpts from those chapters. Reference to "classroom" can be extrapolated to the camp situation. Remember, your discipline must always be with "dignity" (Appendix Figure 3). When we go through a "typical day," some of our rules will become crystallized.

How does the counselor go about "presenting" his philosophy, "typical day," rules, enforcement techniques, etc. to his charges (namely, the campers)? Well there are some really effective times. The best is in the morning of the first full day of camp. This usually takes place after the first full night of camp. Have the kids sit out on the grass and go through your entire lecture. The camp season is young and the kids are not yet loose and relaxed. Hence this may be a time when you will get your best response. Also, they must become acquainted with your requirements as soon as possible—before any negative behavior begins to take hold and solidify. Get your whole presentation out at this point during your morning lecture. During that first evening of camp however, make at least a small speech. The kids are tense and very impressionable at this moment. Just give them a somewhat brief delivery at this point. I'll never forget my favorite counselor's first words on the traditional first evening: "You play ball with us, and we'll play ball with you," i.e., you cooperate and so will we!

What about enforcement? Remember, always—discipline with dignity! Never any corporal punishment. No horseplay, no arm squeezing—no physical contact. No restricting of food or anything of that nature! First you try to reason with the guilty camper—a one on one chat often works wonders. Sometimes I would remove some minutes from the camper's free play time. However, whenever I would remove play time of this nature, I would require that the camper enter into a learning discussion with me and/or fellow campers to last the equivalent number of "docked minutes." I never punish by requiring, for example, the writing 100 times of "I will never throw food again." I would require, however, discussing reasons why food shouldn't be thrown or even essays addressing the issue. Sometimes I would have a "Good and Welfare" (see Chapter 24). At times, my disciplinary methods just did not work. For those times I must use my advisors for their guidance: my groupleader, colleagues, the head counselor, the camp director. The camp administrators may further suggest parental contact or psychological referral. The latter is usually undertaken by the administration! Try never to get too frustrated—there usually is something else to try and in the end you usually do succeed. In the Appendix, Figure 4, are some of my <u>classroom</u> enforcement techniques—extrapolate to camp!

In camp, rules become more crystallized when you go through with your campers, a typical day from A to Z, from Reveille to "Taps." In Chapter 11, we'll go through a "typical day" and see where our rules come into play.

Let's elaborate further here by referring to The Web. As we said, we brainstorm to develop our rules. We do the same when we seek solutions. Jot down all ideas that pop into your head. Network with everyone to get further ideas. As mentioned, always try to reason with the guilty camper (who has violated a rule) on a one to one basis. Use group discussion strategies as well. Through values education lessons and the use of the media, we can bring to the kids examples of good behavior. Also, use role models to address the kids about good behavioral practices. Embedded in your rules should be your philosophy of discipline. In other words, before you even begin to brainstorm, think not only about what rules you want established, but quite importantly—how do you plan on enforcing them? What is your philosophy on this? If you spend quality time with your campers, you will develop such strong bonds with them that you may not even need enforcement techniques, for the kids will respect you and your rules so much that they just won't dare violate them. "Seize the opportunity" (at the moment) at all times to point out and work on negative behavior. Don't let too much time pass in this regard. Again, when all seems to be failing—never give up—first remember that patience and perseverance are essential. Also, that as you gain more and more experience, your rules will not only become more fair, reasonable and appropriate, but your enforcement techniques will also become more refined and ultimately, as we said—you may not even need to enforce your rules—ideally, they just won't ever be broken.

Still, if you seem at the end of your rope—remember—call for help—it's there—just read Chapter 4 to find out what to do!

As mentioned, for school, I have developed a set of 35 rules to cover nearly everything, with a "ladder" of enforcement containing 9 different steps that can be used to solve problems. For your particular camp, activity or bunk, you must also develop your own unique set of rules. Add and subtract more or less, as is necessary. I have enclosed excerpts from my teaching life and the book I authored, "Just Let Me Survive Today" (again, see Appendix Figures 2, 3, and 4).

So, rule composition and enforcement can be considered to be a complex art form. Yet it is, of course, of extreme importance.

4

Never Give Up Hope—There Are Always Solutions

Very often as a counselor, you reach a point where you simply do not know what to do. For example, your disciplinary techniques just do not seem to be working for a specific youngster. You've tried reasoning, as well as various different educationally sound and human-relations oriented punishments, yet nothing seems to be effective. Well, here is where a special form of networking comes in. It could be implemented for any problem, not just camper disciplinary dilemmas.

First, try asking your counselor colleagues if they have any suggestions. Perhaps some staff members have had success with the particular camper or with a particular problem situation (be it anything). That might be your initial step. Then you might need to go further: There is your groupleader. Most camps have an administrative hierarchy. Usually the group leader or unit head would be your first stop for guidance. He often knows a bit more about various situations that will help you to tackle a given problem more effectively. Discuss the given quandary with him. Often fresh insights and more possible solutions will spring forth from the discussion. In fact, most often, the problem will be solved at this level. In addition you will learn another disciplinary technique and your "experience bank" will begin to accumulate more knowledge.

If the problem persists, as it will at times, it becomes necessary to go up the ladder of solutions to the next level—the head counselor. Most camps have a very experienced educator in place at this level. The person usually possesses vast experience in dealing with all sorts of problems. In addition he probably has connections to lots of additional data relating to the problem situation. You and/or the group leader will then brainstorm with the head counselor to find solutions. The problem may need to proceed to the camp director—who is often the owner. These "higher-ups" will have access to parents, doctors, psychologists, psychiatrists, general medical specialists, etc. The point is, it is essential that you network and brainstorm to develop solutions to seemingly unsolvable problems. It is also essential that you never give up trying to solve a problem. Keep plugging away, trying to put together answers to your dilemmas. There is always another person to ask or another conversation to have or another thought to "kick around." Naturally, some problems are very difficult to solve. But through hard work and creativity every problem can be resolved.

Some of the really serious problems which seem so difficult to solve do get to this step. In other words, the head counselor or owner/director may deem it necessary to involve the parent and/or staff psychiatrist. Because of its seriousness, this of course is a problem temporarily out of your control. All the parties involved at that step will brainstorm and discuss (hopefully asking for your input as well) in order to arrive at a resolution that is in the best interests of the child and the camp. That is, some problems are just so serious that your techniques, no matter how superb, have really no chance to work, because the problem may require this more advanced state of solution. Don't feel bad, because some problems are this serious. Hopefully, resolution shall ensue and the camper will return, "all-cured", to your realm. The director and his expert staff of advisors are there in order to solve these knothole (very difficult) problems. In addition, I will often refer to this chapter over and over again. Note that the chapter itself is also a Web component.

It's of such import because again, it shows that often, no matter how good you are as a counselor and at problem solving and disciplining, there will be situations far beyond your control—situations that can only be solved by people having access to more information or only by involving parents and consulting staff psychiatrists. Most often, resolution of even the most difficult of your problems can be effected at this level. Remember too, that on a lesser level, you have your colleagues, groupleader and head counselor to help guide you to solutions which you just couldn't come up with single-handedly. And that's a beautiful way to problem solve!

5

One Often Needs Great Patience

When I was a young camper many years ago, I was a problem for my counselors. First there was the water: I did not know how to swim, and I had an enormous fear of the water. I spent much of my time trying to "get out of" going swimming. I faked being sick, went to the health center almost daily and basically tried all ploys to get onto the so called "no swim" list. In addition to this, I was homesick—most of the time. I cried very often and daily pleaded with my parents to take me home—through phone calls and letters home. When they refused, I tried to enlist the help of relatives or family friends. Nothing ever worked! You know, I really liked camp; it's just that I had these problems with separation. It is also ironic, isn't it, that someone who was so homesick growing up would wind up spending 24 years in summer camp. Perseverance works in strange ways!

Now why did I begin this chapter describing my camp history? I try to illustrate to you counselors out there that you may have some very frustrating times with your campers. You will need to possess great patience. There may be some long, frequent and frustrating conversations with some of your campers:—you may be working with kids who have deep-rooted problems, as I had with separation. Though you may not be Freud, there is a lot you can do to offer support and comfort to your kids who might be conflicted. Just be there as an advisor, as a shoulder to cry on and as a key component in your camper's support network. This is a difficult, challenging, yet often rewarding part of your job. You can try to help the camper achieve one of his (or her) most important goals—becoming independent, self-confident and self-reliant. Some of his fellow campers may try to poke fun at and embarrass the homesick or troubled kid. It will be your job to see to it that all the youngsters are protected from this kind of unnecessary abuse. Of course, each step of the way, you should be in touch with your supervisors, always asking for advice and counseling from them. Remember, Chapter 4 is where to go when you don't know where to go—or what to do—next. As discussed, a good camp has access to professionals from the psychological community "on call" for guidance with thorny problems of camper psychological distress—even for cases of acute homesickness, to mention just one.

There is great opportunity here for you to encourage camper mental health. Don't miss the chance!

6

How Great It Is (Or Can Be) To Be A Counselor!

I believe the job of camp counselor provides an enormous opportunity to the young man or woman who undertakes it.

It provides an excellent chance to make some money in a fun, "outdoors-y" situation. It also gives the worker a chance to experience a job that requires and teaches a) leadership, b) responsibility and c) integrity. One gets the chance to deal with campers, administrators, colleagues, and others, in a pastoral, summery atmosphere. One can really hone their human relations techniques here.

What about these kids? You touch their lives. You spend extensive amounts of time with them. You really get to know them, their thoughts and their feelings. Your influence can help change their lives for the better. They will grow, in part, to be well-functioning adults with great integrity and high moral character. You can help to "undo" some of the problems that may have arisen in their "outside of camp" pre-summer lives.

Some of you might want to go into teaching as a career—or even become teachers in the corporate community, for example. Many of you also will want to get into parenting—as in having kids of your own. Camp—counseling will provide incredible opportunities for you in these areas, with its requirements and demands that are often quite similar to those in teaching and parenting.

For example, as a parent, you have to deal with: a) your child's medical needs; b) disciplining him (or her); c) his (or her) overall problems and needs; d) simultaneously coping with your own problems needs; and e) getting time off for yourself. These issues are "built-into" the camp counselor's job.

You get to deal daily, on all emotional levels, with your campers, your colleagues, and your supervisors. You thus get to practice human relations techniques on many different levels.

Where else can one get all this experience and opportunity for growth under a warm and appealing summer sun? Not many places. The director of my camp often used to wisely say:

"You may not make great money in camp counseling, true, but you do supplement your income big-time with a "psychological salary" that can be worth over 1000 times more than any "real" money."

7

Individual Problems

Individual problems. They can be endless! They range from bed-wetting, to sleep-walking, to fighting, to bullying, and a whole lot more in between. Each is a special, unique situation and must be handled case-by-case, in a unique, individual way—because no two situations are exactly alike. However, in each case, there are a certain set of guidelines that can be applied rather universally. This especially takes us back into Chapters 2, 3, and 4. In almost every case there is much that you, as a general counselor can do. You can bring your own sincerity, kindness and common sense to try and work with the camper. However, in many cases, referral of the case to your groupleader is often necessary so that he (or she) can help guide you in the situation—i.e., give you advice and further input. Depending on the seriousness of the problem, the head counselor and camp director should be kept informed of the progress of the problem. As mentioned previously, every camp should have on staff a consultant psychiatrist who will be able to advise (in many cases) the camp director on how to proceed in a given situation, so that the well-being of the camper is always protected. Many cases can be handled at the above step one, i.e., by you alone, but many need the expert intervention that only further assistance can supply.

For example, one year at camp, we had a child that defecated in bed nearly every night. You can imagine the response of bunkmates, counselors and other parents. What to do? Send the camper home immediately? Let him stay? How do you deal with the various factions here? Well, this of course was a serious case. The staff psychiatrist was briefed on all parties involved and got a handle on the history of the child and his family (with permission and cooperation from the parent of course). He then was able to recommend a course of action appropriate for all involved. The possible consequences to the mental well-being of the camper from being immediately banished had to be weighed against the consequences to his bunkmates. Of course, the situation required great sensitivity, tact and expertise! Eventually, the camper did go home but not without every angle being considered from every aspect by every professional on staff. The health, both physical and mental, of all involved was, and is always the overriding factor of import in all decisions. Fortunately, the camper returned a few weeks later, his apparently temporary problem (caused by certain stresses in his life at that time) ameliorated. He was then able to enjoy the rest of the summer and the other kids got a lesson in understanding, sensitivity, maturity and tact—one which they will always remember. The point is, serious problems require serious help, and it should always be available. Serious decisions should not be whimsically made.

What about the "bed-wetter?" This is a common problem that must be handled discreetly. Try to change the sheets when no one is around. Reassure the camper not to worry—that these kinds of accidents are a common part of growing up. Keep up with business as usual. If anyone gets involved in teasing—cut it off immediately and have a long talk with the teaser not only about the harm that he might be causing but also about his need for increased sensitivity. Make all the kids aware, as a group, that everyone is going to have some problem or other at various times in their lives and it is important to always treat each other with respect, understanding and sensitivity. Here again, keep in touch with your supervisors to help monitor any situation. In the rest of the book, if I write "refer to Chapter 4" for further guidance, then I essentially mean that you should keep both your groupleader and head counselor in touch with the situation at hand, and, that if necessary, the director, parent and staff psychiatrist might be consulted as well.

Eating problems can often rear their ugly heads. They can take many different forms and our ladder of referral must often be employed. For example, I had one camper that had frankfurters for <u>every</u> meal and the chef actually had specific instructions from the parent to carry this out. Another camper had peanut butter 90% of the time—including at breakfast. There are enormous numbers of problems that can be food-related, and that eventually can reach into higher echelon difficulties—those of anorexia and bulimia, which can be life-threatening illnesses. For most food peculiarities, consult with your supervisors, who, in turn, may need to consult with our staff of experts. When in doubt—check it out! Many food problems, especially anorexia and bulimia, may have roots in childhood disturbances (some minor, some major).

Still on the topic of food, we do have the "bunk slob." The slob may be like this simply because he has not been taught well at home. Or perhaps he simply "wants attention." Well, he can be taught proper techniques of etiquette, which you will be inculcating to your campers on a daily basis. Your charges can be taken to eat with other groups or on field trips to restaurants and local homes to observe good manners. If it's attention that is needed, he'll get it from you in a positive way (right?) so perhaps he won't crave it in this unhealthy way. When all else fails, consult Chapter 4. But remember, very often, kindness, understanding, one on one talks, group rap sessions, tact, common sense and discipline with dignity shall negate any need for a consult with Chapter 4.

Here comes the bully—the pit bull kid. The bully seems to have the need for picking on his bunkmates by verbally or physically abusing them. He (or she) wreaks emotional havoc on his victims. Here again, it is important that you try to reach the aggressor via multiple methods: Consult The Web: one to one talks (on his level of understanding) to try and reason and teach him why it is unhealthy for him to keep up this barrage; group talks; all the myriad inputs from values education and its lessons—which will have a powerful effect on changing negative camper behavior of all kinds; bringing in guest speakers and other role models to help exemplify positive behavior traits; influential pieces from the media—some great videos and movies are out there; field trips to appropriate locations where positive values can be learned; the use of a strong set of rules that you have communicated to your kids with realistic and effective enforcement techniques. Again, this varied approach is how many of these problems can be ameliorated. Not necessarily (but hopefully) solved but at least improved. It might be rather difficult for you, in two months, to solve a problem that probably has deep roots and has been growing for a long time. To undo this damage in two months would be asking quite a bit. However, you can at least make a start toward the necessary solution. The parent will see these initial positive changes (for a given problem) and, being encouraged, hopefully, will continue the healing process when the child returns home. You, therefore, can be the catalyst for change. This is very important work that you're doing here. Again, solving these problems can not be accomplished in any one way. Another powerful factor is created by your tapping on the relationship and emotional ties you have established between your campers, yourself, the administration and the camp itself.

It is only by using this entire combination, this arsenal, depending on each unique situation, that will spell success or failure. And again, success doesn't mean total problem eradication. There is a famous quote that goes: "A journey of a thousand miles begins with one single step." Be patient, persevere, keep trying different combinations and you will succeed. Here we were speaking about the bully. But every problem can be dealt with by these same methods. They do not seem so magical, but when you see the results, you might think magic has been performed. You can truly turn your camp into a Magical Kingdom in this way for your kids.

Here comes Mr. (or Ms) Victim. They seem to be the target of all sorts of abuse: name calling, physical abuse, being "made fun of." Essentially, they serve as the "whipping board" for not only the bully, but also nearly everyone else. Even the counselors seem to want to launch attacks. Why? Well this kid apparently has the need for this kind of treatment. It seems "normal" to him to be abused. When he is treated with respect he feels very uncomfortable. Perhaps he has been treated poorly at home and this treatment makes him feel at home, safe, secure. When he is treated as a king he gets a large attack of anxiety and homesickness and he will do anything within his power to restart the abuse—and he's a master at it. He knows just which buttons to push in everyone. He's probably been doing it for years. Well, the game is over now, and you're onto his strategy. You might be the first to be ever "up" on his plan. But you're also the one who's going to put an end to his misery. You're going to set him off on his 1000 mile (and maybe it won't be so long) journey toward the goal of increased self-esteem, self-respect and comfort with his new position—his new home. No longer will he be homesick for that old, worn out, broken down, inadequate and inappropriate home that he had once lived in—the home with walls decorated with lack of self-esteem, the home with dilapidated carpets, broken windows, and inadequate heating. He has moved to Buckingham Palace and you know what—everyone around him will soon quickly learn of his new address and will now have to make an appointment with his secretary instead of just busting in unannounced whenever they please! Our visitor has become King and no one is ever going to step on him again.

How do you set him off on this journey? By going through each component of The Web, we will review the procedure for problem—solving success. For each problem that you encounter, the "Web of Solutions" (from now on referred to simply as "The Web") must be consulted and its component parts implemented so that its powerful results can be attained. Review Chapter 2 on The Web at this time.

Let us now return to those individual "problem-types" that we had been dealing with.

For example, the "shy" child. This camper is extremely quiet—very rarely speaks. As usual, learn anything you can about your children's background that may help you understand the etiology of the problem. Perhaps the head counselor, director or parent might share with you some insight into the problem. Look over The Web and try to creatively come up with solutions. Tap on its various aspects to help you out. For example, you might want to do some "one on ones." Appropriate role models, the use of values education and further input from

Chapter 4 might help. You might want to try getting the camper involved in some activities that might help to "bring him out of his shell": becoming an announcer at an all-star game or a reporter or editor for the camp newspaper. Spend some "quality" time and find out just what are the camper's major interests. Then get creative and let the Web "do its thing." Remember again—patience. That long journey is about to begin. Perhaps the child has been living in the shadow of an older, very successful sibling. Perhaps the parent has not encouraged self-expression and has supported this kind of creative suppression. You may never find out the definitive reasons (for the problems), but you can sure start trying to work the "magic" that you now know is capable of working! His parents and teachers may be in for a (hopefully) great surprise when summer ends and his self esteem has grown 300 percent (or more) thanks to you and your professional, caring ways.

Homesickness—this one is the all-time most common malady of camp kids. I suffered through this condition for many years at camp. For me, as mentioned, the roots were probably in the separation anxiety (from home) that plagued me in camp. I was a child of a very overprotective mother and this made normal, healthy separation, for me, quite difficult. I was always trying to leave camp and get home. Even though I spent much time crying, I can say that I really did enjoy camp—on some level—after all, I did return 24 times. In fact, even as a counselor, I, at times, had that homesickness anxiety that I had to deal with. You know, there are some teachers I know who dread going to school in the morning—not because they don't like teaching but just because of the anticipatory anxiety of the unknown events of the day ahead. This dread might result in throwing up, even on a daily basis, or in other stress—related illnesses. The point is, some of these problems can be adult-sized and they're being dealt with by just (often) little kids. They need us to be on their side to help them to do battle (and become "Warriors") against these fears. They need our support, our time, our shoulder, our sensitivity, our friendship, our caring. Again, the reasons for their particular version of homesickness may be enormously varied: They have overprotective parents; they may have separation issues, be immature, and not be "ready" for camp. They may be: "Victims" of bullies; apparently not be a "right fit" for that particular camp; ill too often. In other words, again, the reasons may be multiple. To solve, "hit" The Web. The sensitive counselor must do lots and lots of one-on-ones here. The staff member must be sure that the other kids don't pick on the troubled child. Instead, the astute counselor will try to encourage the youngster to get involved in very interesting activities or with very kind and supportive friends. A keen interest in some activity may be the necessary button to push. Use your creativity and sensitivity! This particular condition often takes <u>extreme</u> patience and perseverance. Experience also will help you to deal with the challenging problem. Perhaps more than many other problems, the techniques of Chapter 4 will be necessary here. Almost for sure, you'll need advice from the administration, who will be in touch with the parents. But you know what? Probably you, your techniques and strategies and your creative ideas on solving this problem will be the best hope of finding the solution! <u>You're</u> the first line of defense and in this case, probably the <u>best</u> line of defense! Of course, this problem must be closely monitored, because, unchecked, it can lead to constant crying, depression and even "running away." That last one, of course, can be quite serious and every effort must be made to prevent it. Any danger signals that arise (and they almost always do) must immediately be detected, acknowledged and dealt with very seriously. Again, all administrative levels should be alerted to the existence of a homesick child.

Fears. Fear of the water (of swimming, drowning), fear of animals, fear of the dark, fear of the woods. These are just some of the fears felt by some campers. And these anxieties can be very uncomfortable and overwhelming. I should know—<u>I</u> suffered with these problems as well. There are fears for just about everything under the sun—including fear of the sun itself—of sunburn, cancer of the skin, eye damage, etc. It is not my purpose here to get into the solution of every problem—but hopefully, to help you to realize—perhaps by now—that the solution to all of these problems requires a somewhat similar strategy—and this strategy is essentially located in Chapter Two—The Web. Let's take, for example, fear of the water. Let's take a look at our Web. One on one discussions between you and members of the waterfront staff will help. Group discussions on techniques of swimming will allow the camper to start getting acquainted with some of the methods of swimming and water safety. He will begin to realize that many kids can safely swim and that it looks like fun. Lessons from values and outdoor education may further help to dissipate some of the fears. Swimming role models will certainly help the camper to progress. Videos and movies on swimming will help the fearful camper further begin to see that the reality is that swimming can be a joyous experience. The input of Chapter 4 is again essential. Perhaps there is something in the camper's background that might help you to better understand and conquer his fear. Still, to those of you who have suffered from phobias (myself included), we know that a phobia is often an irrational fear and that these techniques, although palliative, are not necessarily curative. Perhaps for this one, what is needed most is the Web input of "Patience, Perseverance and Experience." First you need the talents of an experienced swim instructor—one who's been through all of this lots of times before. Add to this enormous patience on the part of all involved and a tenacious desire and never give-it-up attitude of great perseverance possessed by all: camper, instructor and counselor. The support and sensitivity of a kind general counselor or groupleader will also go a long way toward a successful outcome. All these ideas will, hopefully, in time, help to chip away at the phobia or fear of the water. At some point, with all this help, the desire to swim will become greater than the fear of the water, and a happy group of participants in this emotional struggle will celebrate an enormous victory.

Sometimes it takes a unique event or happening to explode a phobia. I was afraid of dogs all my life—would often cross the street to avoid them. One day, when walking quite slowly with my elderly father, I was attacked and bitten on the leg quite severely by a Doberman on the loose. It was my worst nightmare come true. I received a tetanus shot but you know what? Nothing serious really happened to me. Again, the reality of my worst phobia had come true and I was still alive to talk abut it. My phobia very quickly began to dissipate. Usually though, it may take a long time to overcome one's fears. A supportive staff of understanding counselors will go a long way toward finding the cure. At times, professional counseling may be needed to deal with the phobic behavior.

We have the hypochondriac camper. This is the child who always seems to be ill or not feeling well. Again, I refer you to The Web. This multi-faceted attack on any problem is, as usual, the superb method of choice. You know it by now. First, check out any background information (see Chapter 4) on the child that may supply you with necessary insights into the problem. "One on ones" will help. Group discussion on good health habits would be another input. Values education including lessons on personal health care habits, video and media pieces, guest speakers (doctors, child psychologists), and puppet shows on appropriate topics all will help to get the camper thinking about good personal health management techniques. Scanning The Web we also call on "minute by minute" opportunities, and your own uniquely creative ideas. Of course, as usual, patience, perseverance and experience are all essential. At any step along the way in your brainstorming, problem—solving procedures, you may want to again stop and call on "the teachings of Chapter 4," because this (or any) problem might be beyond your scope and you may need the immediate input of the "emergency" techniques of this important chapter. Hopefully, this camper will be, at the end of the summer (or earlier), near the culmination (or close to it), of his possibly thousand mile journey to being at peace with his health status. Again, solving some (or many) problems may be far beyond the scope of the camper's capabilities. Long term solutions may be needed from the home. However, whatever assistance you can provide here would be, of course, extremely valuable.

There are many other "typical" problems that can be dealt with using the procedures in The Web. Go around this "circle of solutions" and use one, a few, or all of the suggested areas surrounding the core of "successful problem solving." Remember, every problem is unique, and for the same problem, different campers will present you with (possibly) totally different procedures for dealing with an issue—since each camper, is of course, a totally unique living individual, with totally individual needs and attitudes.

Among the virtually hundreds of other problems that will face you during the summer are: the camper who doesn't want to play sports, or for that matter, do any activity; the campers who tend to form "cliques" and snobbishly exclude many from joining; the accident-prone camper and the camper who must deal with a recent change in the family—a new brother, a new parent, a parent who has just passed away, a divorce in the family. I could go on and on with this list. However, I hope I have provided you with a basic framework for dealing with virtually any problem. The methods are similar. Proceed with a caring, human-relations oriented, sensitive, networking, kind, loving, motivated, creative, insightful approach to every problem and issue, and you will succeed magnificently as a summer camp counselor, educator and human being, and you will be a hero to your campers, peers and supervisors. The psychological salary you will earn will make the yearly salary of Michael Jordan look like peanuts in comparison. Your personal journey will be well underway. Good luck to all of you!

8

Shtick and Mishigos

At the camp I worked at I was a waiter, a general counselor, a groupleader, an assistant athletic director. However, in every role I brought with me a unique style that made me "special." I know I'm bragging but this is partly what has made me unique and successful both in education and in camping. My camp director used to say: "Mark, I don't care what you do in camp this year, be it general counselor, athletic person, etc., I just want you to be in camp with all of your creative "Mishigos" that can be applied to virtually any activity or area in camp. I am a big believer in the "show business" aspects of education. We must compete, here in the 90's, with the internet, movie special effects, etc. We must put on our own special show, we must motivate by exciting and stimulating. And believe me, it can be done! Always look for the unique angle. Know what excites your kids and work on doing it.

As far as "Shtick And Mishigos" is concerned, please refer back to Chapter 2 for its working definition. Basically, it is creative comedy with motivation as its goal—motivation to do almost anything. We elaborate further in this chapter.

All of what is mentioned in this chapter takes planning, brainstorming, rehearsing, organizing, trial and error, risk-taking and experimentation; the ideas presented and discussed (as well as many from your own unique imaginations) will succeed—but only through hard work and effort.

When do we implement our Shtick at camp? Any time is really the right time for Shtick and Mishigos! Implement it while the kids are on their way to activity, in the dining room, at free play—at just about any time! However, there are certain times which "give" to the use of Shtick and Mishigos: rainy days, evening activities, free play and regular activity being the main candidates for its implementation.

Let's first focus on activity period as a prime time to "spice up" an event. For example, as an athletic staffer at camp, I always tried to mimic "big league" ball as often as possible. During exercises and warm-ups, we tried to replicate pro-drills.

Also, kids have a fascination with "stats" (statistics)—which is often at the heart of all sports. So, during games like baseball and softball, I kept stats—re: batting averages, home runs, game-winning hits, pitching victories, strike outs, etc. In basketball, soccer and every other sport, stats were also kept! This gives rise to awards—league leaders, gold gloves, MVP's, most improved, best sportsman (and woman), purple hearts (for duty beyond the call—i.e., diving for balls and often sustaining injuries—hopefully minor ones). Also, announcements at lineup, trophies, prizes, other awards, banquets, team recognitions, etc. are generated thusly. Players vote for and participate in all-star games. Level "B" players are also recognized to encourage their efforts. All of this stimulates enormous interest. I kept standings, had playoffs, World Series games, etc.

"Stat" sessions are arranged where campers are trained in stat calculations. The kids love to keep score and use their newly-acquired knowledge of these calculations to help in record keeping. Some of the "lower level" athletes, not chosen to play, help with stats and managing and coaching during all-star games, etc. Encourage participation by everyone in some way. Bring on internet use for the 90's and beyond.

During all-star and playoff games, for example, mimic the big-league process as much as possible: have a national anthem, conduct interviews for the camp newspaper, have publicity photos taken of the stars, set up autograph-signing tables, retire uniforms, have players line up on the field a-la the World Series, create team songs and cheers, take team "road trips" to other camps, have 7th inning stretches—the possibilities are endless. At all-star games have home-run derbies, lay-up contests, half-court million to one competitions, slam-dunk fests (at lowered baskets), street hockey one on one shoot-outs. For track, swimming and hoops, have many different types of one-on-one, head-to-head competitions. Every event should be publicized with flyers and fan-incentive for coming (giveaways). Hold some of these events during free-play, rest hour, hobby periods, evenings, any time. As we see above, don't stop at baseball—use every sport and camp area as well. Use your creative juices to come up with exciting angles on this issue.

For more specificity: at the softball (baseball) all-star game, the various team members are announced over a long-speaker or megaphone. They trot out onto the field and line up for the National Anthem along the first and third base lines. As they are introduced, they go down the line slapping high fives as they go. The fans, who may have (depending on how you set it up) voted on the player selections, are providing support in the bleachers. The MVP for the game is selected and at the conclusion of the event, the post game show is conducted in the dug-out by camp reporters. Anxious fans line up for autographs outside the locker rooms (bunks) of the competitors.

Other unique competitions could be held: The 3 on 3 hoop competition, where, for example, a team consists of 2 guys and 1 gal. However, if the girl scores, the team is credited with 3 points rather than one. Games are scheduled and publicized far in advance. It can be implemented as single or double elimination, or as a "ladder" (like in tennis) tournament where when you beat a team above you and exchange spots with them on the ladder. Top runger eventually is crowned champion.

As previously mentioned, you can organize a half court shot competition where various prizes are awarded to those who sink this very low probability shot. You can conduct full court basketball one on one competitions, beach-volleyball one on ones, etc.

The point is, the possibilities for these little competitions and events are endless. These little pieces of Shtick ("shticklachs") are incredibly effective in generating and "souping up" camp spirit, which is an essential component of successful camp life! You can have the kids compete in virtually anything—flag raising speed, bed-making speed, speed of brushing teeth and putting on pajamas and of waking up and getting out of bed, dressed and ready to go in the AM. Unique prizes can be used as further motivation. Always be on the lookout for stirring up spirit in this way.

Crazy, silly (mishigos) activities are not limited to the ball field. Let us go on now! How about my patented "How to be Cool Course" (Appendix Figure 7). It is effective with kids of all ages. In my course, I run a given workshop thusly: I might be demonstrating one of my "cool walks" (one of many lessons). I show all how it is done. I usually demonstrate some very cool (but silly) walk that I do and I then call on volunteers to try it. I give pointers to them as they go through their motions. Everyone then gets a chance and they are sent off to practice. The younger kids really think it's great fun, and the older kids think that it's so silly and ridiculous that it becomes "cool." My cool course has elevated me to cult status in camp and school. Richman? He's just so-o-o cool! The cool course, which I also use in school, has been an incredibly powerful tool for increasing spirit and motivation as well as simply for just having fun. It is unique, special, creative, and highly "mishigossy." Since it is included in my book "Just Let Me Survive Today," as mentioned, I have included a further description of it including application for it in Appendix Figure 7. Check it out!

It is now time to take the methods illustrated in this chapter, and apply them to the evening activity program. Therefore, when you read Chapter 12, please refer back to this key chapter.

9

These Moments Are Special
(Prom, Olympics, etc.)

During the summer, there will be a series of events that will stand out from the rest. These are those major galas, parties, ceremonies and happenings that are extra-special—some of which the kids (and counselors) will keep in their golden memory banks for as long as they live.

The first of these is the solemn "Opening Campfire." It is a ceremony steeped in camping tradition. The campers are welcomed and introduced to camp, its customs and many of its key personnel. All the while, a beautiful campfire is burning in the foreground. As citizens of the camp listen to the welcome wishes, they are able to and encouraged to "look into the fire" and reflect on the upcoming summer with all of its wonderful potential. Talk with your kids about this philosophical notion of "smelling the roses." Sit down with them either before and/or after the evening ceremony to discuss and share feelings in this regard. Teach them the power and healthiness of self reflection and analysis. Help them to try and make every moment in their summer have a meaning, a purpose. This is another of your gifts to them. A wonderful tradition at my camp—Trail's End Camp—had its roots in this activity: At the closing campfire of the previous summer, a group wish was made by the members of that summer season. The wish was written down, sealed in an envelope and buried in a chest in the ground, only to be covered, over the winter, with the snow and ice of the season. It was then dug up and read by a staff representative at the subsequent opening fire. It was a really nice touch and a beautiful experience, especially if the wish was relevant and meaningful. The wish was usually presented by a staff member with a booming voice that would melodically echo through the warm summer air. At the conclusion of the campfire ceremonies, campers, as was often done, would sing "Friends," and hear the sounding of "Taps." Teach your campers early on the meaning and significance of these songs, and be sure that they do not use them as opportunities to "get silly" at these events. Many camps also have a traditional "camp song" that is sung at serious and poignant moments like these. Stress the importance of the often meaningful words and/or feelings inherent in many of these songs. To me, "Taps" was a bugle that was a signal to end the day in a clam, peaceful manner with silent reflection. For me and my campers it was also a time to reflect upon those men and women in the military who had given their lives, spirits and passions to defend their country, our country. Right at the beginning of the summer, I always would impress upon my campers that at all times, there would be zero tolerance for disrespectful attitudes and actions. The opening campfire also provides an excellent opportunity to set a tone for your group. It is their first major activity and you can start explaining and implementing your philosophies and expectations at this activity. Usually the campfire would end with the entire camp facing one direction, where a burning sign saying "Aloha'98," for example, would appear. Campers were then escorted back to their bunks and were prepared for their first evening (ever for some) away from their parents. In Chapter 3, we explained the power that exists in this first night with your charges. Always be alert for severe cases of homesickness at this time and be ready to use your sensitivity techniques in dealing with the problem.

The closing campfire can be looked at in one way as a mirror image of the opening campfire. There are, however, a few differences. There is probably not going to be any crying over being homesick—the crying here will be because of impending separation from friends of the wondrous summer experience. This campfire is thus always a very moving experience for the children. It serves as an end to a wonderfully emotional time. For some it will be the first time that these feelings have surfaced. At the closing fire, each group individually made a wish for the future campers, and all the wishes were also sealed in that container for the following summer. High caliber representatives from the current season are the ones called on to orally make these wishes (The format can be varied). At the conclusion of the evening, one final rendition of the "Friends" song, the camp theme song or Alma Mater, and the sounding of "Taps." A flame is lit spelling out, in a unique arrangement of burning logs: "Until '99," (or the subsequent year). The point is, no matter how your camp chooses to do it, one final gathering like this is an extremely important stop. Again, as campers return to their bunk areas, keep in mind that this will be one last chance to solidify the emotional bonds that have been formed between camper and camper, and camper and counselor. On this final evening together, all counselors should be "on duty" and should take advantage of this time to talk to their campers while the lights are out and the kids are in bed. Perhaps conduct one final 'round the bunk "good and welfare" session. Let the kids express their feelings. Prepare a meaningful "closing address" to them and include all of your feelings as well. Deliver it to the campers. Have your co-counselors have their say. Make plans for a camp reunion. Again, this is a wonderful opportunity for exchanging deep feelings.

Another major event is "Olympics." Traditionally, many camps have similar activities, such as "Color War." However, an Olympics provides a superior opportunity to teach—to teach sportsmanship, teamwork, perseverance, spirit, love of sport, caring for friends, physical training and so much more. The "real" Olympics have so many of these ideas and concepts simply "built in" that it makes great sense to pounce on these existent components and use them effectively. The Games should start with a "break." Olympics are usually a culminating summer event. Hence, it occurs mostly toward the end of summer and usually lasts for 4 full days of competition. Longer duration might become too intense. The "break" is the point where the event begins. Usually some sort of unique event triggers it—for example: announcements are dropped from planes flying by—pronouncing, "This is Olympics!" or, a diver holding a sign "This is Olympics," emerges from the lake when the entire camp is assembled there. Several "false" breaks add to the great anticipation. Large booklets are eventually distributed to campers containing the following information: team membership, i.e., who is on what team; a full day by day Olympic activity schedule for each group, with point values to be awarded for each event; rules for each event; a brief history of the Games; and a statement and description as to the meaning, significance and importance of the ideals of the Olympic Games. This is a monster event for the camp season. It is a highly emotional period and has extreme value.

In keeping with the fine tradition of the "real" Olympic Games, there is an "opening ceremony" (culminating in a solemn campfire). The three nations dress up in their team (color) uniforms and there is a "parade of nations" as with the real Games. Captains and co-captains are chosen and these folks provide leadership and team spirit. They are outgoing counselors of high energy and integrity, always keeping their team members focused on having fun—hopefully winning—but mainly zeroing in on those ideals that the Olympic Games really stand for—fair play, effort, friendship, teamwork and integrity. They keep the spirits of their team up no matter what the overall "medal standings." They give motivational speeches, come up with charismatic cheers and even write poetry to honor their team's heroes! Good leadership will go a very long way to a successful Olympics. Choose your leaders wisely!

What can you as a general counselor (non-captain) do to ensure the success of the Games? Again, always try to stress to your kids the meaning and significance of the Olympics—that sportsmanship, courage and integrity are numero uno here! In the heat of the Games there are some "danger" signs to watch for. Some of the campers will take the events too seriously and have difficulty handling adversity and defeat. They will become depressed, angry, or will strike out at their teammates, coaches or opponents in very unhealthy ways. These children will require the teachings of The Web. Other problems that might arise are overexertion and overtiredness, heat debilitation, exhaustion and other physical and emotional disorders. To solve these and all problems, reach out to our Web. Begin by brainstorming—just what do you seek as your ultimate goals of these Olympic Games? Set your philosophy of "The Games." One to one pow-wows with the camper in distress are quite helpful. Keep him focused on what really is important! Group and team discussions and strategy sessions, under your leadership, or that of the team captain, are vital. By using role models out of or in camp, the children can further feel for the meaning of the Games. The media-magazines, videos, movies, you name it, are over stocked (especially during "Olympic" years) with information and points of extreme interest and timeliness on the Olympic Games. In fact, in my book "High Caliber Kids," there are specific lessons from the realm of values education (see excerpts in the Appendix Figure 11) based entirely on Olympic events. Of course, at this time of summer, as at every other, enforceable consistent rules on all aspects of camp must be maintained and enforced. These rules might have to be modified perhaps somewhat for the Games, but flexibility is always a key component of disciplinary guidelines. An "Olympic" argument breaks out in the bunk: "Your team is the worst!" and a fist-fight seems imminent. Well "Seize the Opportunity" and perform an Olympic-sized values lesson right on the spot!

Quality time spent with your campers at such an emotionally-charged period of the summer will surely not only keep the kids grounded and stabilized but will reap great benefits to your relationship with them. The lessons of Chapter 4 will, as usual, help you to solve those very difficult (as we call them—"knothole-type") problems. Patience, perseverance and experience are the glue that often tie together your philosophy, goals and actions. Safety, of course, must be maintained during the Games. The Games provide an excellent setting for the exercise of your own creativity, especially in the area of Shtick and Mishigos. Go creative! After selected (any or all) events, you can have medal ceremonies with the playing of national anthems. There can be interviews with the Olympic Stars by the camp media-newspapers and camp radio station (if it exists—and if not, why not start one?). In the evening each team gathers as a group, discusses the day's events, honors its heroes of physical prowess and those of moral strength as well.

Each team develops a march and an alma mater and they are rehearsed nightly and presented on the final evening—where, with the entire membership of the Olympic Village in attendance, speeches are made, heroes are honored and a (point) winning team is announced. However, the entire camp membership is truly the winner. The Olympic Games is the epitome of a camp culminating event that will bring out the best in all. It will be a week that will last forever in the hearts and minds of the participants!

The "Prom" or "Final Dance" is another huge, "special" event! It is the culminating social function of the season. Of course, during the summer there are lots of "small proms," that is, lots of social gatherings for campers (of all ages) on a much smaller scale. However, the basic idea behind all of them in the same and will be the topic for discussion in this section. At the prom, the kids all get dressed up quite nicely and the room where the dance is to be held has been beautifully decorated during the preceding 12 or so hours. It is a really wonderful event and can be very exciting. I believe in the philosophy of a co-ed camp. I believe that the socialization afforded is extremely important. Try to "talk up" the prom and seek to make it as non-threatening as possible to the campers. There should be no "pressure" on anyone in any way. In fact, some camps require camp uniforms to be put on at the prom in order to cut down on any clothing competition. Let's examine The Web for the prom. First, as usual, brainstorm with the staff about the priorities at your prom (and all social events for that matter). Jot down notes and organize them. This exercise should reflect your philosophy in this matter. Mine would be that everyone is to try and enjoy but be sure that no one gets hurt, put down, humiliated, embarrassed or made fun of in any way and for any reason—be it poor dancing ability, or poor anything. Everyone is made to feel good and enjoy. Everyone is cordial, friendly and kind. There shall be zero tolerance for negative behavior toward anyone. Along these lines, practice one on one and some group discussion to be sure egos are kept in healthy shape with high self-esteem and self-respect being paramount. During the summer there are always opportunities for appropriate "values education" lessons, such as those in "High Caliber Kids." The media provides fabulous videos, movies, and songs on socialization, "mingling" with the opposite sex, dating and growing up. Role models such as "big brother and sister" types can certainly lend an encouraging word and ear. At all social events of this nature there must be reasonable rules to ensure the safety and well-being (physically and emotionally) of all parties involved. Experience is the best teacher for all of us who've come through the socialization process, and we must teach our kids patience and perseverance. How many rejections do most guys (and gals) experience in their dating years? Most of us lots—and we must help our kids learn to patiently deal with the inevitable rejections in a positive and healthy way. This, we, as educated insightful and sensitive counselors, can do—and do magnificently. We all know of the critical importance of helping to protect and nurture the developing self-images of pre-teens and teens. What a rough age it could be in this regard! We can provide the essential support so necessary here. Every moment can provide us with a snapshot "Seize The Opportunity" teaching minute. In this entire scenario, add a dash of your own unique creativity, mix, stir, stand back a step and watch these kids blossom! As usual, the campers will know when your efforts are sincere and when you're just punching the clock and can't wait to get away. At times, depression and very negative feelings may begin to develop in a youngster with a fragile self-esteem. When your methods don't seem to be succeeding, don't despair—consult Chapter 4—and of course never give up hope. We mention the safety aspect. Remember, campers are to be supervised at all times—they cannot run off to be alone. Use discretion here. Consult with your groupleader and head counselor now (and always) when you need some advice. As far as prom and social Shtick and Mishigos, get creative! Have freeze dances, dance contests, best dancer competitions, etc. Students may record rap (or any other types of) music that they have composed. Light refreshments or major food can be served. You can have a costume party or perhaps you can dress up as Elvis or even Elmo.

So again we see that a "cigar is not just a cigar! Every camp event (including this one) becomes a Super Bowl, a World Series, an Olympic-sized gold medal, a Stanley Cup Final. It all depends on your leadership qualities, organizational skills, motivational techniques, courage and creativity. You can make it both fun and educational to the fifth power.

Let's now hit the "rubber chicken" (banquet) circuit.

Another big event is the banquet. Many of these really big events seem to occur at the end of the summer—and thus they are "culminating" activities. However, during the rest of the (earlier part of the) summer, similar or other uniquely interesting activities can be arranged by the "brainstorming" minds of a wonderfully charismatic and super-creative staff bent on injecting some excitement, fun and Shtick and Mishigos into the summer program at every turn.

Let's return to the banquet for a moment. This is a super culminating event—a veritable festival of food, good feeling, entertainment and "honoring." First of all, the best meal of the summer is usually served. The banquet begins at around 5 pm on a day approximately 3 or 4 days before the end of camp. It can be compared to a combination of a gala wedding, bar-mitzvah and sports banquet all rolled into one. In between courses, or at the very end, the festivities begin. There are speeches by many staff members and campers. Awards in the form of trophies and certificates are distributed to deserving and successful campers. In this way, it mimics an Academy Award presentation. And done well, it can generate as much excitement. Then, performers from the various dramatic presentations of the summer are called upon to reprise their big hits as the crowd relives and recalls those magical moments of a now waning summer season. Many years ago, the banquet concluded with the enjoyment of Baked Alaska cake. In addition, there was a procession of waiters marching around the dining hall, each holding a soup tureen full of flaming "cherries jubilee" that would eventually serve as topping for the delicious cake. Oh what a night! What can we learn from this discussion? Well, first, again, that these big time events truly make for major camp memories. And you can design your <u>own</u> original, unique, major event at <u>any</u> time during the summer! It doesn't have to be an opening or closing campfire or a prom, banquet or Olympics. To design your event, start by brainstorming and note taking. Gather your thoughts and ideas—organize them. Discuss your ideas with all members of the camp community. You've turned to The Web. Examine every other component. This will give you that framework which you need to construct an effective plan. Rehearse it. Refine it. Discuss it. Implement it. Like magic—a major fun event can be created to add to the already rich traditions of your camp. A few points from The Web that are appropriate here in this case. Always have your philosophy behind your planning. This gives your event a purpose, a meaning, a soul. The discussions will help you to enlist support for your ideas and help to maintain it once it is "alive." Public relations and promotion is of extreme import. Call on role models and the media (including your own camp media system—newspapers, bulletin boards, etc) to help generate interest in your particular special event—be it banquet, prom or some new event. Even an off-season camp reunion can be effectively planned in this way. Always be sure your plan is accompanied by a reasonable set of enforceable guidelines—for example, at the banquet there needs to be rules for the behavior of participants, for the arrangement of tables, order of the show, type of food, etc. At any moment, a teaching opportunity may suddenly present itself—a nasty comment is made, a camper loses his temper, becomes sick, receives good news, bad news, etc. Seize The Opportunity! Remember we're here to teach. For every event, your own unique style is what you bring to the camp and the kids. "You are special!" as Barney the Dinosaur says—and don't forget it! Let your ideas, creativity and unique style come through—and try to ensure that the campers have the same spirit. Remember, <u>you</u> are a 24 hour a day role model. Whenever you run into problems in any way in planning your big day, remember there is always hope and help—reread Chapter 4. After you implement a given event once, you become a veteran and the experience you gain will make the second event (even another new one) seem so much easier. You can be a Trail Blazer, which by the way was the name of my camp's (Trails End) newspaper. When things start to fall apart (or if you think they might), persevere—never give up. And don't forget to add a dash of patience. Don't be too hard on yourself—or your kids. Remember, you're experimenting with new ideas and new practices. Enjoy! Of course, for every new activity or event you pursue, there must always be consideration of Safety and Shtick and Mishigos. First we mention safety. In planning for your new event, consider all of the safety aspects that need attention. Do a "walk through" of the event in your mind. Try to account for every possible little item (no matter how obscure you think it might be) that might go wrong, and have a strategy to deal with it, so what seems to everyone to be a safe and smooth-running activity (and it really is), really arrived at that state because of the great planning you performed to make it all happen. And of course, we never must forget "Shtick and Mishigos."

In every activity, there is often the need for some comedic, creative, "wild and crazy," uniquely special way of thinking and as a result, a reflected method of implementation. In every activity there should be injected some form of charismatic input: It's Abbot asking Costello, "Who's on First?" It is the uniquely special performances of Elvis, Michael Jackson, the Beatles, Mick Jagger, Billy Joel, J-Lo, Fifty Cent, Eminem, Jessica Simpson and Bruce Springsteen all rolled into one. It is the Mets winning the '69 World Series, it is the Islanders wining four Stanley Cups in a row; it is Mohammed Ali winning the Heavyweight Championship and Billie Jean King defeating Bobby Riggs. It is Lou Gherig delivering his "Luckiest Man on the Face of the Earth" Speech and Babe Ruth sadly bidding farewell to baseball. It is the miracle—like performances of Joe Namath in the '69 Super Bowl, guaranteeing victory over the 19-point favored Colts, or the "immaculate" reception of Franco Harris for the Super Bowl bound Pittsburgh Steelers. In the World Series it is Mickey Owen dropping a 3rd strike, Don Larsen pitching a no-hitter or Reginald Martinez Jackson smacking three home runs in one game. More recently, it is the Yankees winning the '96 series (and then many, many more) under the comeback kid Joe Torre, whose brother simultaneously was having a life-saving heart-transplant. It is "Winning One for the Gipper." It is the charisma of Vince Lomabardi, George Allen, Mike Ditka, Larry Brown, Phil Jackson, Bill Parcells, and Connie Mack. It is Cooperstown and the Hall of Fame. It is Jimmy Stewart on Christmas Eve in "It's a Wonderful Life." It is Michael Jordan. Period. These are just a few of the many examples of charismatic performances that in one way or another can be used as a (inspirational) springboard for ideas that can be turned into "Shtick and Mishigos." In other words, grab the feeling, charisma, spirit and uniqueness of these one in a lifetime events and situations, and bottle it up for a bit. Then, when your creative brainstorming has come up with some idea that you think has great potential, open up your bottle of spirited charismatic magic and let it penetrate your idea, giving it life and magnificent energy. Your ideas will now mushroom into incredible creations which will enliven the spirits and lives of all who are involved. Are you beginning to get in touch with the nature of a "Shtick and Mishigos" possibility? In any event, this is how we put together a "Special Event" Package—from Campfires to Olympic Games to Banquets to Proms to Anything. In fact, as we have discussed, small events can be turned into gala happenings as well. Some other major events bear mention.

One is "Sing." This uses as its basis the "Sing" activities that are so prevalent in high schools across the nation. It is an event that can generate enormous spirit for the bunk, group and camp. By using The Web as your guide, you can plan for an effective "Sing." You can include campers themselves in the composing of group songs and related shtick. There is great enjoyment that can be shared by a group singing event of this nature. You will be thrilled by the excitement that can be generated. It will provide for the strengthening of group bonds and will be a whole lot of fun.

The group basically rehearses with their co-ed counterpart group and each division comes up with a series (usually 3) of songs—a march, alma-mater and folk song. Groups are judged on different aspects of their performance and an overall winner is declared. Often, costumes and "acts" are part of the presentation. At first there is usually a "Do we have to practice again?" attitude amongst the kids, but as Sing Night approaches, even the most resistant-to-practice camper is usually caught up in the spirit and excitement of the (almost like opening night on Broadway) moment. Everyone wants to win. This is a great activity for team-building and spirit. In referring to The Web for Sing, we do have some of the usual learnings from it. But also, let's highlight some Web components unique to Sing. Creative brainstorming is a big input of the activity. Public relations helps greatly to promote Sing to the camp. As Sing Night draws near, group cheers in the dining room begin to bloom like tulips in springtime. Your group discussion and one on ones help to stimulate enthusiasm. Since "Sing" is essentially a show-biz activity, "Shtick and Mishigos" creativity can play a big part here. In addition, "Sing" requires the creative energies of every member of the camper and counselor community.

Carnival is another huge highlight of summer. Basically, each group sets up two booths—such as a "douse the counselor" or "shoot out the candles with water-guns" activity. The various booths are constructed, set up and attended to by camper and counselor representatives. Campers who partake in booth games get little "tickets" or "coupons" if they win—which later are turned in for small prizes. There is a tumbling show early in the day and there is a food booth where campers can get soda and hot dogs. In other words, it is a traditional "carny." It is an absolute incentive for bringing out all of the creative juices of the camp community, not to mention brainstorming practices and a big opportunity to employ "Shtick and Mishigossy" ideas.

So again we see that the number of special events has really no limit and that these very important activities add to the growing treasure chest of golden camp memories.

Why not have an Elvis Day where everyone dresses and acts like the "King." Or perhaps a "Barney-Day," or "Sesame Street Day," where everyone does anything that your creative mind comes up with. Let those juices flow!

10

At The Activity—All Of Them

Each unique area in camp comes with a special, unique set of guidelines, rules, procedures, method of motivating and desired outcomes. Much is a reflection of the camp philosophy as well as your own philosophy. Let's see how this all plays out at each individual area at camp.

As mentioned in Chapter 6, we have the unique opportunity, in camp, to be able to teach youngsters many important values, among them: teamwork, sportsmanship, caring and integrity. These values help guide us at all areas of camp life.

Let's zero in, for example, on the explosive sport of the nineties—basketball. We refer to the ever present Web that we have discussed so often. It can be used as a springboard to this Chapter as well: for example, on the court (of hoops), we often begin with group lessons (and discussions) delivered by the basketball specialists. He (or she) gives instruction and sets up drills. The other staff members can serve to assist him in organization of the practice sessions. Often this is all supplemented from one on one instruction from any qualified adult present. "Seize the Opportunity" moments can come up at any time—those instant teaching moments when one camper, e.g., yells at another and puts him down. Call a time out; pull the combatants (or at times the whole group) over for a quick lesson on some aspect of values education. Of course, sports areas provide golden opportunities for assistance offered by role models (pro athletes or even older campers who are held in high esteem by the particular group) who can help to model admirable skills, behavior and attitudes at the given area. Still working with The Web, enforceable, reasonable rules must be presented to the participants—usually during their very first time at the activity. For example, food and drink may not be permitted onto the court. The sport might require special outfits (whites for tennis, bathing suit for swimming, etc); behavior must be of a certain quality conducive to learning. What if a player is feeling ill or the heat is getting to him? Rules are to be understood by all involved. Quality time is that taken by the counselor to work, perhaps one on one, with the "struggling to succeed" youngster, who will never forget this personal attention afforded him by his A+ counselor, while the D- and F staff member is off shooting hoops on his own, totally ignoring the camper who needs his help. He (the failing counselor) might then wonder later on, just why doesn't this kid listen to me when I ask him to do something. The important teachings of Chapter 4 are, as usual, called into play if you are dealing with a camper with some rather serious problem, like: a) refusing to play; b) constantly fighting with his group mates; c) becoming severely injured while playing, etc. In other words, you may, at some point, need to "network out" to get some solutions to seemingly insurmountable problems. Remember also those Web components of patience, perseverance and experience, which, as always, will serve as pillars of strength and courage to help get you successfully through tough times!

In using the Web, you are free to use, of course your own special creativity and ideas to enhance the camp program in a given skill area. Freelance, enjoy, create! Make a name for yourself—start your own camp tradition. Become a legend!

The final Web components here at activity are Safety and "Shtick and Mishigos."

First Safety. At all areas of camp, staff must always be extremely safety-conscious. The camp should have an overall safety plan with fire-drill procedures, etc. However, at each specific activity there are certain unique items of which to be wary. At basketball, for example, brainstorm for possible dangers: The court is wet or has debris on it; the balls are not properly inflated; the backboard or rims are loose; the support for the backboards are not properly padded; campers are running up and down the court with laces untied; a thunderstorm is eminent; it is too hot to play; campers are not properly protected from the ill-effects of the sun; teams are highly unequal as far as ability, which possibly may lead to an injury to one of the participants; play is getting too rough; there are too many potential fights. These are just some safety hazards for just <u>one</u> activity area. It seems rather overwhelming and difficult!

Let's discuss more about safety! Of course you do not want to get too overprotective, but for each area, you (and the activity specialist and camp administration) must have safety guidelines established and be ever vigilant. One severe injury can ruin the summer for everyone. The kids can still enjoy the activity, but never forget that you are entrusted with the lives and safety of your kids. This is obviously a huge and important responsibility. Rise to the occasion! Your future parenting skills are also being honed in your role as counselor.

Now, we are not going to cover every camp area individually. However, the same techniques that are applied to basketball are also applied to hockey, tennis, the waterfront, baseball, softball, volleyball, track, riflery, archery, horseback riding, and arts and crafts, everywhere. In other words, first tour The Web touching on each and every appropriate component. Eventually, move to the area of safety. Brainstorm and compile a full list of hazards that all must be aware of. Compile your list in collaboration with the area specialist, the group leader, the head counselor, the parents, the director and even the campers themselves. Safety itself can be networked via Web techniques. Now, before we turn to highlight a few other activity areas, let's look at the "Shtick and Mishigos" aspects of the given activity area.

Let's continue here with basketball. Reread Chapter 8 on "Shtick and Mishigos." In this chapter is found many techniques on motivating youngsters at the various activity areas. For example, at basketball, the campers need to be exposed to exciting incentive activities to maintain their high motivation. You should run all sorts of competitions: one-on-one contests; three-on-three and five-on-five half and full court competitions; three-on-three co-ed events. These competitions should take place at regular activity periods, free plays, hobby periods, as evening activities, etc. See the Prize Chapter (22) to check out the possible awarding of prizes. This is always a very big motivator. Consulting Chapter 8 we see that some of the events (which are discussed there in more detail) are: all star games, playoffs, slam-dunk competitions, old-timers games, autograph-signing sessions, wearing team uniforms, and more tournaments. One can generate the same excitement that is seen for the NBA Playoffs and even the NCAA Tournament. All stars are voted for by the fans (campers) or by the players themselves. Stats are kept for all activities (by camper statisticians trained in the computer/calculator techniques of the 2000's). Why players can even have agents (Jerry Maguire) and be a part of a "Draft." Can you see the possibilities?—they are indeed endless, limited only by your own creativity as a teacher and motivator.

So you see—you have a tremendous amount going for you at each activity. Begin by brainstorming for ideas. Use The Web to guide you. Don't forget to zero in on the areas of Safety and Shtick and Mishigos to ensure the health and high motivation of your campers at each activity area.

You can use the framework above to deal with every area of camp but let's just hit on a few right now to highlight important aspects of the given activities.

First tennis. We brainstorm and consult the Web, including Safety and Shtick and Mishigos. You come up with your personal tennis agenda. At tennis, besides the usual concerns, you must be extra careful for sun and heat safety. A word about these items. Actually, similar concerns apply to every outdoor summer activity! The sun, of course, in summer, is extremely hot. Campers must dress accordingly and always protect themselves with hats and sunscreen. Counselors must be vigilant in this regard. Also, it is important for the active camper to keep himself well—hydrated with liquids so that dehydration or heatstroke—related problems do not occur. Great patience is required with the tennis playing novice because this can be a very frustrating game, especially for the littlest athletes who often have extreme difficulty hitting the ball effectively. Creative games and practice strategies must be invented so that probabilities for success of some sort are high—otherwise frustration will set in and the game will quickly be dropped. Ladder tournaments are great for tennis—whereby one player challenges another above him in a ladder—style arrangement, and they exchange places after respective wins and losses.

Golf is another area that has similar pitfalls as does tennis, but it, too, can be spiced up via hole-in-one contests, miniature golf parties, etc. Videotaping of athletes can be a successful instructional technique which also provides fun and motivation.

The waterfront is an area that requires special mention here. It, of course, may very well be the most dangerous area in camp. Why? Because an error here might result in fatal consequences. Hence it is extremely important that the director of this activity issue a set of strict safety rules that must be followed to a "T." Down here, when on duty, there can be no "fooling around" or daydreaming by staff. Campers must have "buddies" and a system of accounting for them at every second must be in place. It is not the purpose of this manual to give a set of water safety rules, but as a counselor you must always realize the importance of good on the job safety practices—especially here at the waterfront area. For fun, swimming can be motivated by races and swim meets, stats and awards. Again, high-quality sun protection techniques need to be practiced here.

There are many areas of the camp activity scene that remain to be considered: volleyball, softball, baseball, hockey, track and field, horseback riding, riflery, archery, arts and crafts, and much more. So I am now sending you all off on your own highly creative paths. It doesn't matter what activity I speak of now. You know the procedure. You know how to succeed magnificently at each and every activity. Look at the Web. Brainstorm! Put down your initial ideas on paper. Plan your strategy. Cover every aspect of The Web. Employ "Shtick and Mishigos!" Have fun and be creative! Be unique and charismatic in your approach. Remember, you must stimulate enthusiasm in your charges. Be sure to include all the safety strategies also, as needed!

Let's throw out a few tidbits for some of our aforementioned activities: at volleyball try one-on-ones or three-on-threes on the beach; at hockey have one-on-

one shootout showdowns between goalie and offensive goal scorers; have horse shows if your camp has horseback riding, replete with medals and ribbons; the list can be endless.

Publicize all events and activities via the camp newspaper, by announcements at lineup or in the dining room, on camp bulletin boards, and by any other techniques you one can come up with.

11

A Typical Day

In this chapter I would like to set out an ideal time schedule—one that I observed almost minute for minute at my camp—for 24 years. Time structure is important—many kids thrive under this regimentation. Flexibility must be allowed for however, as excess rigidity is not healthy either!

Camps have time schedules that vary as far as activities, get up times, rest hours, mealtimes etc. Therefore, this chapter's time schedule, although recommended by me for camps, will not necessarily be the standard. However, it will provide, hopefully, an excellent reference framework for staff to use as a learning guide. Read my dialogue and extrapolate it to your unique camping time schedule needs. Encourage your administration to make changes in your camp timing if you think it warranted.

Let's begin with reveille—the army wake up bugle—call that sounds (on the PA system) at about 7:30 AM daily. Then comes the friendly voice of the head counselor: "Wake up everybody—rise and shine sleepy heads—get ready for a great day." A brief news and weather report can then be broadcast—often by a group of camper—newscasters. Campers then have one half hour from the sound of reveille to the sound of the next bugle call—namely "first call for morning lineup." It is essential that all campers be ready for lineup and are not late. The kids must thus get up, wash up, get dressed and start making their beds. Some campers (and counselors) will want to play Rip Van Winkle at this time. You must get the children out of bed and "rolling" in the morning. Do it by talking with them, coaxing them, even rewarding the most responsible in this area. It is important, as we said, that counselors get enough rest and go to bed early enough, so that they can be able to rise themselves. If not, a poor example is set for the kids.

Well, (as we said) we then have the bugle for "first call" to lineup. This precedes line-up by 5 minutes. Campers stop what they're doing at first call, and assemble on their bunk porches. Then there will come the call to morning lineup.

Campers line up in front of their bunks and proceed to morning lineup for the hoisting of the flag. What about lineup—its meaning and purpose?

At lineup, basically, the boys camp and girls camp (if co-ed) must separate to 2 different locations. There, the entire boys (or girls) camp gets together and "touches base"—important announcements are made, stories are exchanged, the campers all stabilize and regroup!

After morning lineup we proceed to the dining room where our "eating" rules (Chapter 21) swing into effect. Back to the bunks we go for cleanup, health call, inspection and first morning activity call. First comes cleanup. In Chapter 25, we go through all aspects of this key morning routine. Say we're out of the dining room at 8:45. At 9:00 am, health call (via bugle) sounds and campers in need of medical attention proceed to the health care center. Many kids are overly concerned about their health and would go to see the doctor every day if unmonitored. Thus some kind of screening procedure must be implemented here. Campers might be required, for example, to get checked out by their groupleader or head counselor before proceeding to receive medical attention. At around 9:15, the "inspection bugle" sounds and formal inspection begins. The designated "inspector," usually a groupleader, goes from bunk to bunk, checking for good cleanup practices. He rates each bunk with a number—10.0 being perfect and tenths of points deducted for deficiencies. It's a weekly bunk to bunk competition with pride and prizes as rewards. Inspectors should have reasonable expectations and be fair at all times. Fifteen minutes later, "activity call" sounds from the bugle (usually a record) and campers are off to their morning activity #1. The bunks, by the way, should remain relatively neat for the remainder of the day—not to the degree of AM inspection but later in the day, periodic "light" inspections should keep things reasonable.

After inspection comes the full morning program. At about 9:30 or so comes the call to 1st morning activity. Campers line up in front of their bunks and proceed to their activity areas—be it softball, waterfront, arts and crafts, etc. Periods 1 and 2 are usually 45 minutes each in duration. Hard-working counselors again earn their salary here! It is important that staff be awake (here is where late—evening carousing will hurt the kids) and motivated. At all activities it is your job to actively supervise for safety and participation by all. Try to make sure your campers are all involved and motivated. Be sure they are courteous to one another. Here (as almost always) your active supervision is quite the requirement.

As mentioned, the sun can become quite hot and problematical as far as safety is concerned. Monitor the climate. Be sure your kids are properly protected—with hats and/or sunscreen and/or liquids. Be alert to the camper feeling ill, homesick or just not wanting to get involved. Be patient and understanding. Try and creatively make him feel like becoming more of a participant in the activities.

Also, a counselor usually receives one period off per day. Use this time to relax, recharge, and do something enjoyable. Often the periods are rotated so each day you get a different time slot off (see Chapter 13). Return from your period off on time so that there will be no problems with coverage. It always presents a serious dilemma when counselors exceed their allotted off time. Remember, you're here mainly for the kids. You're a professional and have the welfare of your campers as your #1 priority—not your own needs. These will be well satisfied in time also.

The bugle sounds for period 2—often the 2nd half of a double period activity. The end of period 2 coincides with 11 am and it now is time for period 3—often an hour in length. Different camps have different activities at this time. Again, no camp schedule will be identical. However, in this book when I discuss a particular schedule, it is meant to be a framework for any general line up of periods. The primary items are the ideas expressed during our discourse.

As for period 3: An example would be a "hobby" period where campers get to choose any area of camp in which they desire to participate. At each area, the specialists unique to that activity are awaiting the campers who signed up for that spot. This period, although one hour in duration, will have kids participating in some of their favorite activities. At this time (12 noon) in most camps the "recall" bugle sounds—when kids return to their bunks and get ready for lunch. Counselors should see to it that the kids get back in a timely way and get themselves ready for lunch—i.e., wash hands, face, etc. They will have a 1st call and again a lineup before lunch—to regroup and again have announcements, etc. Onto the dining room for lunch, another opportunity to teach manners and high quality eating habits. At this time (right before lunch), many camps have orders filled for "canteen" a kind of snack bar where campers order snacks that are picked up by monitors after lunch. This process (canteen) is unique to the individual camp and will not be discussed in any detail here.

After lunch most camps have rest hour. Traditionally, this should be a time for rest and the "recharging of batteries" for the remainder of the day. Some campers lie in bed, read, play quiet games, etc. This might be a time when counselors can organize a nice discussion group. The counselor must be certain that the kids are at least trying to put in some rest time; in any case, that they are not getting too wild at this point. Some counselors on duty at rest hour often tend to "sack out" themselves. This is not a wise move because rest hour, as all other times, can have its moments of danger, and an unsupervised group can lead to serious problems for all involved. At times campers at rest hour may partake in activities out of the bunk. This is fine as long as there is supervision and purpose.

By the way this can be an opportunity for counselors to showcase their athletic skills in the form of softball, basketball or soccer games. Campers get the opportunity to view the spirited contests, while staff members not involved in the game are assigned responsibility for the supervision of campers in attendance.

At around 2:05 there is an announcement: "There are 5 minutes left until the end of the rest hour; All off-duty counselors (those on "free" time) please return to their bunks." This is the signal to all that cleanup procedures in preparation for afternoon activities should begin. Bunks again will become fully-staffed and the "wheels of preparation" will begin spinning. Rest hour wraps up and campers go through another light cleanup, followed by a cursory inspection. Bunks need not be in a sate of maximum "morning-cleanliness," however, they should not be permitted to deteriorate into "pigsty's" either. Also, campers are to prepare for the afternoon program. Counselors again are there to supervise, motivate and "set in motion."

Well, it is now 2:30 and the first afternoon activity begins. No lineup now—just out to the various areas. Forty five minutes later, activity two begins—again usually a second period of the same activity. What to watch out for in the afternoon are frequently very severe heat problems. Counselors, as usual, must look out for the "sun protection" of their charges. At times, summer heat might become so severe that activities need to be curtailed in exchange for an "all afternoon general swim."

In any case, "general swim," where much of the camp goes for a dip, occurs at the third afternoon activity point. General swim, or any swim time, needs to be a very organized activity where again, the eyes, ears and concentration of all supervising staff must be focused on the water. A mistake here might have deadly consequences.

After swim comes "return to bunk" time. Campers return to their cabins for showers and preparation for dinner and evening activity. Once again, careful supervision is essential at shower time.

At shower time, campers often get into various types of "horseplay" situations—like running on wet floors, like snapping wet towels at one another, like wrestling around sharp pointy objects, etc. So here, as at all other areas, staff should be ever safety conscious.

When campers complete their showers, it is time for some "free play." This means that the children may leave the bunks and play outside in the general vicinity, use swings or use any other equipment that might be out there until "first call" for dinner, at around 5:45 pm. Thus, when pupils finish their showers, they're set for free play. However, we again want to ensure bunk cleanliness. How so at this time? Well, let's discuss the timeline for a moment. Campers are back for showers at around 4:45 and they are concluded at about 5 PM. This is a good juncture for "mail call." Of course, the kids love receiving and reading mail. So, after showers, children get dressed and straighten up their beds, which by this time of day tend to look really badly. It is also a good time for them to give their morning jobs a quick once—through, especially those in charge of the bathroom and shower areas. Require then that the kids be "checked out" before they are allowed to receive mail and go out for free play. This means that the camper comes to the counselor and specifically asks to be "checked out." The counselor inspects the child's bed, cubby area and job quality, and when they are found to be satisfactory, the camper receives his mail and is permitted to go out and play. This way the children learn much about responsibility: They must put their possessions away and keep neatness as a priority. There must always be good "coverage" at this time. Counselors must be inside the bunk to supervise shower/ cleanup/mail time as well as outside to orchestrate free play and to be sure safety procedures are followed at all areas.

How about this "free-play" period? Campers are free to enjoy this time. Counselors often can use this period to get closer emotionally to their charges. They can play ball with them, have "catches", sing songs, talk, in short, do anything to encourage those intimate bonds that can be strengthened at this opportune time. Free play at this point must be restricted to the bunk area and not to all over camp, i.e., it is a "local" activity. It is now 5:45 and the first call for dinner bugle sounds. A word about the bugles I describe here. Some camps prefer this regimented army—style bugle sounding philosophy. Others negate the mindset preferring "periods without borders;" in other words, a very loose time set-up. No matter which your camp chooses to implement (or even a combination of both) the basic ideas of safety, responsibility and rule—following remain essential.

At the aforementioned first call campers quickly wash-up and get set for lineup. Five minutes later, the assembly for lineup bugle sounds and campers proceed to the flagpole for dinner retreat. The flag is lowered, announcements of accomplishments and coming attractions are made and the camp proceeds to the dining room for dinner. Again proper manners are enforced as well as techniques for clearing the table and helping the waiters and waitresses (often former campers and "pre-counselors") do their job more efficiently. The dining room is always a fine scene for the singing of spirited camp songs—usually around dessert time. Announcements are made at the conclusion of dinner and campers are often sent out (it is about 6:30 pm now), for free play all over the camp. Counselors are assigned to various posts for the activity and again, supervision and safety are of major priority here. Sometimes "challenge" games, all-star games, etc. take place at this time. It is a nice period for socialization and fun. Usually, at around 7 pm, the recall bugle from free play sounds and campers are directed to return to their bunks to prepare for evening activity.

The schedule is never identical each day, or each evening. Again, this simply reflects an "average" day.

So here we are at recall from the evening free play activity. Campers return to their bunks. They "freshen up" after free play, and the first call bugle, as usual, gives them the 5-minute to lineup warning. "Lineup" is then sounded and campers assemble at their respective areas for brief announcements. They then proceed to the evening activity. These activities vary by the day. Scheduled can be campfires, hayrides, sing downs, movies, talent shows, family feuds, sports events and any number of other items. Some of these activities may need such extensive blocks of time that evening free play is eliminated and campers begin their night program much sooner. The program should be varied as much as possible. At each unique evening activity, staff members again are presented with the chance to educate their campers in the specific behavioral objectives of each particular endeavor. For example, at dances, social skills can be worked on. At campfires, campers can learn to philosophize and reflect as they look into the rising flames and burning embers of the summer campfire. Talent shows provide excellent opportunities for camper self-expression, self-esteem building and fun. The point is that each evening activity, or any activity for that matter, provides a special creative chance for staff to enhance and improve the lives of the children under their potentially powerful guidance capacities. See to it that your kids get the maximum learning and enjoyment out of every single activity and you will truly be a hero to your campers.

As all good things must come to an end, so does evening activity. Campers are escorted back to their bunks to prepare for bed. They hustle back, get into their pajamas, wash up, brush teeth, and neatly put clothes away or into their laundry bags. Here again, the practice of bed—time rituals can be inculcated. Many are not well—schooled in this particular area of life. Another golden opportunity for you at this point, with the great skills of the counselor in getting their campers to quietly and safely get to sleep being called into play. We now thus refer you to Chapter 24, which will effectively "take over" from this point through to dreamland.

Hopefully this lengthy walk through of a (possibly) typical day should serve as a framework for you to sort out the structured nature of a day in camp life. Your particular camp might vary greatly from this description, might be far more or less rigid and structured. However, <u>some</u> sense of organization and structure must be built into any effective program and you must be able to convey this structure (with guidelines and rules) to your children, for without it, there will be chaos and complete lack of discipline. So sit down and map out an outline of what is a typical day for your unique situation, your specific camp. Go from dawn to slumber time, write it out (as an outline if you prefer) and convey it to your campers as soon as possible so that they know what to expect and what you expect from them. Communicate often with them. Respectfully tell them when they're not meeting your standards of behavior and when their attitude is deficient. Talk to them individually and as a group. Never give up on them! Of course, every day need not be a typical, boring, drone-like, "cookie-cutter" duplicate of every other day. Variation is the spice of life in camp as well. Just keep that general skeleton structure as a flexible guide to you and your kids.

Let us briefly mention our Web with respect to a typical day. In setting up our day, we brainstorm and take notes on what we will be requiring at every moment. We need to account for every minute. Our rules should be reasonable and enforceable. They are developed in consultation with everyone. One on one and group discussions are needed to get the routines across to our kids. They need to know exactly what we expect! Veteran campers and current administrators can be used as role models to help set routines. Experience will teach just what important guidelines are for our typical day, and if you do not have any, there are always veteran camp people to help out. Perseverance and patience are necessary in all areas of camp life. Your developing philosophy and that of the camp should always be inherent in the spirit of what you do and how you organize. My philosophy of education (as discussed earlier in the book) is essentially similar to that for camping.

Your own uniquely creative "fingerprint" should be evident in your presentation of a "typical day." Of course at every moment there will be uniquely available "teaching moments." Seize the opportunity! In putting together your moment by moment day, seek help from your supervisors and other camp administrators, and—especially if you're having any difficulty—read chapter 4! So much (and it was a lot) for a "typical day!"

12

Evening Activity Primer

At this time, it is important that you review Chapter 8, because these two chapters (8 and 12) really go hand in hand!

As chief organizer of evening and rainy day activities, I often called on a "Talent Show" to help out. This can be done camp-wide, group-wide or even bunk-wide. You get together a bunch of kids who want to perform—and encourage this artful expression. Have tryouts, but in general, have everyone who wants to be in the show in it. The kids get super-excited and look incredibly forward to their moment "in the limelight." Make sure that you rehearse often and that each performer knows exactly what they're doing. See to it that they practice on their own. Make sure they'll be reasonably presentable (and not get "the giggles"), which nearly everyone who wants to, can be. Get everyone together and give them a pep talk. Tell them to work hard on their act and to practice a lot. Warn them about the (remote) possibility of a rude audience. This should not be a problem because right at the start of the summer, you will speak to and teach the audience good behavior. You must do some rehearsing but this kind of show usually "runs itself." You need to make up an order or agenda however. Planning this is essential. Put the acts in a reasonable sequence—comedy, vocal, dancing, etc., rather than 3 comedy acts, e.g., in a row. Do not place multiple acts with very young performers in a row. Vary the order—type of act, age group, etc.—use your judgment. Conduct interviews with the performers between acts. For pointers on this technique—an excerpt from one of my books can be found in the Appendix in Figure 8. Before this and every other type of performance, make a list of "props" that are needed—what each specific performer requires—and be sure to have everything set to go before show time.

Let's digress for a moment and discuss show planning in more detail (which really correlates to all planning). Always sit down, brainstorm, and make an outline of what it is you want to do and how you plan on doing it. Consult The Web for further guidance. Account for every minute and aspect of your show or event.

Get all your necessary needs together (organize them into a chart or list), whatever they may be—props, touching base with someone, scenery design, etc. Plan every step in your mind and then on paper.

Rehearse the show—first totally in your mind, and then actually walk through the plan yourself and finally with the entire cast. Try to enlist assistance. Use children (and staff) as "monitors" or "helpers" so you will not have to work on everything alone. This planning technique can be used effectively for shows, special events, mishigos, etc. Very often you will have to make speeches before your campers, the entire camp community, the administrators, parents, visitors, anyone. This same technique can be used effectively for its organization too. Sit down with a pad. Brainstorm. What do you want to say? Jot down notes. Make an outline—order it. Refine it. Add to it. Rehearse it. Rehearse again. Bingo. A great speech! You can even put key ideas in order, on index cards, and present your speech with a great amount of eye contact. So we see, that to present a great speech or organize a great show, requires lots of behind the scenes preparation.

Now let's get back to some <u>more</u> show and special events planning. Where can one get lots of great ideas for activities and games? Everywhere, but let's specifically discuss a few. First is by networking out camp wide. Ask the campers and counselors for suggestions. Often great ideas begin in this way. Also you can network with other camps—via conferences, inter-visitations or even the internet. Great ideas can be exchanged. Also there is TV. Some of the greatest "gameshow" minds have created many super quiz shows. Before camp (or during), sit down (alone or with "consultants") and watch some game shows. Try to use them as a springboard to launch you off on your own creative path. They may touch off ideas of enormous power.

For example, a great evening activity I used to run was one of the multiple versions of the "Dating Game". Gentlemen (or ladies) are given a prepared set of questions (many of them quite humorous). The gentleman asks these questions of the 3 (hidden from his view) ladies and then he chooses one for his "date" (a chaperoned event appropriate to the given age group in question). The camp loves this kind of cute interaction with all of its possibly funny and unpredictable responses. Again, you need to do a lot of planning—creating interesting questions, enlisting funny and outgoing contestants, writing up an effective script and having all your props prepared. You must always be sure (in advance) of an effectively operating sound system. Any breakdowns here will result in a very flawed performance and unhappy audience.

Then there is "Family Feud." Teams are composed (in advance), questions prepared, a game board assembled, "buzzers" secured and rehearsals performed

(Consult Appendix Figure 9 for a description of how I run some of these game shows and shtick events in the classroom and this should be of help to you in organizing for your particular camp situation). Make it very similar to the TV game show. You can also use "The Price Is Right," "Jeopardy" and many other TV quiz shows and creatively adapt them to the camp setting. Again, the possibilities are endless, only limited by your own desires and creativity.

How about a "Singdown?" This is another great camp activity. Again great planning is necessary (as usual). Teams are made and they are placed in various sections of a (large) room. A word is then given to the teams—for example, the word "green." Teams must come up with as many songs as they can that contain the word "green" somewhere in the song. Songs like "Greensleeves," "Green Grass of Home," "Beautiful Green Eyes," etc. are prepared to be sung by each team. When the judge points to a team, the team has 10 seconds to begin its singing. Points are deducted if only some members of the team are participating. Solos are performed by some team members.

Another idea is "theme days." For example, on "Elvis Day," campers are encouraged to dress up as the King. Elvis songs are played on the loudspeaker all day. Elvis decorations abound in camp and Elvis history readings and stories are told. The whole day takes on an Elvis theme. Or, you can have Michael Jordan Day, Beach Boys Day, New York Knicks Day, Shaq Day, etc. In the Appendix Figure 10 I present a lesson plan illustrating the technique of Elvis Day that I use at my school. Adapt to your camping needs.

A brief mention of other, more traditional evening activities. After dinner and free play, activities can often take the form of: hayrides with singing and laughing, bowling parties, roller skating (to music) nights, casino nights, dances camp-fires and scavenger and treasure hunts using wild and crazy charismatic clues. So these traditional camp activities often with a dash of (90's and 2000's) Mishigos added, can be instantly transformed into unique evenings of unforgettable happiness. Camps also often include days or evenings devoted to (the appropriate) religious observation.

So to summarize, we see that camp spirit and enthusiasm, which are essential, must be generated, and techniques of accomplishing them often come from creative methods employing Shtick and Mishigos. So, every time is a great time for Shtick and Mishigos! Think show—biz—make the kids laugh. Create! Have a ball!

13

Boy, Do I Need A Break—Counselor Free Time

Time off for staff is extremely important. There are days off, evenings off and periods off. Counselors need rest and relaxation away from the virtual 24 hour on-duty job.

Let's talk first about days off. Besides the rest that it provides, change of scenery is of extreme importance. Many counselors on their days off hang around camp to partake in and enjoy the camp's facilities. I do not recommend this except maybe for only a few hours. It seems OK in theory but when your day off is over and you return to work, it can be as if you never even had a day off.

Now what to do on your day off? The possibilities are endless and of course everyone has their individual desires. Let me relate some of the things that we and others did on our days off. Often, staff took the opportunity to return to home or school to see family, friends, etc. Beaches in the area or canoeing adventures were possibilities. There were mall-shopping, movies, summer stock, local hotels, day-trips, restaurants, local tennis and golf spots and so much more. Find out what's going on in the area; get local guidebooks to help with your planning. Then go off and enjoy-relax, and rest. Some counselors were known to rent motel rooms for the day just to sleep or to use as a base of operations away from the kids.

There are some problems lurking out there for the off-duty staff member. One is cars. Very often, counselors do not have them and this creates problems—cars are often borrowed and this can involve difficulties. Of course, sometimes, there just are no autos available. When this is the case, camps can provide buses or taxis or staff can pool funds to hire "wheels." Whichever method is employed, safety concerns must always be at the top of the list. Often camp roads are dark, winding and dangerous. Factor alcohol into this formula and disaster is often the result. This, by the way, especially applies to evening time off. Quite often, after the kids are put to bed, counselors bolt for the local "watering holes" to have "a few beers," and unwind. Again, the dangers from driving on unknown roads with a "full tank of booze" cannot be overemphasized! Please be careful and use "designated drivers" at all times. Wise camps directors often set up facilities on the campgrounds itself to allow for counselor evening socialization and relaxation.

Some other difficulties often arise when staff is off-duty. One is the use of drugs. Staff who indulge in this activity should obviously be <u>instantly</u> dismissed. Smoking cigarettes in camp should also be restricted. Some counselors engage in what they think to be "fun" activities—at the expense of the kids. Let me elaborate. In the evening, for example, after the kids are put to bed, off-duty (or even on-duty) staff do things like putting shaving cream on the fingers of fast asleep campers. They then tickle their noses. Beds are "frenched" (or short-sheeted) so that when campers insert their feet, their feet are stopped halfway down the bed by the "shorted sheet." There are other counselors pranks that I've seen performed: Spreading "hot" toppings on midnight snack pizzas, waking slumbering campers up for a "sleep walk" and performing numerous other demeaning, humiliating and abusive stunts. There just is no place for this kind of thing. Some counselors are young, immature and out to have a good time—at the expense of the kids! This cannot be tolerated and if observed—it should be reported and guilty staff should be fired! In summary, enjoy your free time. Relax, rejuvenate—but be careful, stay safe, and don't do anything unwise or unprofessional! The kids need you and are counting on you. Do not let them down!

14

The Precamp Camp

I cannot imagine a camp beginning without a "Pre-Camp." Now what exactly is this? It is a period of time before the children arrive when only staff members are in attendance. An ideal period might be 3-5 days and actually the longer the better. Its purpose is extremely significant—to prepare the (often "rookie") staff for the summer to come with all of its ramifications. Counselors, mostly teenagers, are to become full-time parents and are going to be asked to discipline, teach, organize, plan, and mold. These tasks are nothing short of monumental. A crash course in these issues must be performed over this pre-camp period. Also, counselors are given the opportunity to set up all of the camper "stuff" so that when the kids arrive, they're set to go—their clothes are neatly put away, their shoes are lined up, toiletries set out nicely, etc. In addition, their activities, inspection assignments and everything else are "set" to go. Can you imagine arriving at the same time as the kids? Having your things to square away as well as those of your campers. Utter chaos and disorganization—yet some camps do not have this extremely important session.

Now let's go through this situation in a bit more detail. Let's refer to our Web. First we brainstorm. This is usually done by the camp director and administrators. They generate a 3 to 5 day all—encompassing agenda for what they want to be covered in the pre-camp program. Again, this period is extremely important. Basically, the agenda should include, but not even be limited to: everything that is contained in the table of contents of this manual. In other words, go to the table of contents and include sessions covering <u>everything</u> that is in it, that is, that is in this book. A full program for the entire time period is planned. Of course there will be folks in charge, running the show. Session material will be presented in many forms—via lecture, role-play, question and answer, walk-throughs, etc. The goal is to help the fledgling counselor pick up as much preliminary orientation and guidance as is possible. In addition, camper and counselor clothing must be put away in an organized, neat way. Bathroom supplies are neatly housed in their appropriate areas. The inspection system is set up as is the entire activity schedule. Everything is made physically set to the point of near perfect readiness so that when the first campers arrive, the program is set to begin. Counselors, many of whom are from other countries as well as other parts of our nation, and some of whom have never done anything like this before, will be made as ready as is possible under the given conditions. Back to The Pre-Camp Web. There will be presentations from role models and veteran staff members on procedures, including values education. There will be viewing of appropriate presentations via video, TV, movie and other forms of media. In other words, the entire pre-camp situation will be analyzed, broken down, and the methods inherent in The Web will be used as instructional techniques in presenting the very program itself.

Another huge benefit of pre-camp is in the socialization that it offers to the new staff. Before the kids arrive and all the pressures set in, counselors will be able to share this intensely emotional period with one another, forming friendships, bonds and support networks that will hopefully help them cope with the ups and downs of camp life. They will become familiar with the camp program and choose their areas of special interest. Counselors will begin to from their own personal philosophy for the summer, a process of supreme importance, for with it they will have a guide that will help them to deal with every activity and situation. They will learn techniques of discipline and motivation. Pre-camp will not only provide them with a crash course in counseling techniques, but it will also afford them some free time (albeit not much) to have fun and enjoy the summer's pleasures in a (relatively) ideal, stress—free setting. Staff will have a chance to quiz the experts, have group discussions and learn about individual problems they might be facing with their soon to be arriving youngsters. "Pre-camp"—I cannot imagine a successful summer without it!

15

"Trip the Summer Fantastic" (Camp Trips)

In camp there are often overnight trips that are taken off the premises. Some of them might be simple excursions into the wilderness while others might be several-night trips (via bus, train, or even plane) to big tourist sites—such as (on the NE coast area) to Lake George, Cooperstown, Hershey (Pa), Gettysburg, or any number of other nice attractions for children.

These overnight trips provide wonderful learning experiences for the kids, and once again, you can be the guide that leads your campers to achieve the desired positive outcomes.

First there is the psychological angle involved in "tripping." The kids are leaving the nest and are off on an adventure—of their own. There is that healthy change of scenery.

They must prepare for their journey. The technique of "packing" is taught here. Adults know that readying for trips can be quite a demanding experience. The kids learn how to make packing "lists"—i.e.,—what to take with them. They learn organizational skills in this way. They learn of the importance of planning and "thinking ahead." They must not take too much—they learn to prioritize. If too little is loaded they might wind up being unprepared for various eventualities. They must learn to use these aforementioned lists to organize yet not get too wild with them since some folks can let these tools get quite out of hand at times.

Then there is the camping out experience itself—usually outside under the stars, or at the very least, under a tent.

Upon arrival campers are instructed in valuable outdoor survival strategies—namely, e.g., tent pitching techniques—a valuable skill and a self-esteem builder. What about chow-time? There are new procedures to learn for group outdoor eating—both for you and the kids. You might even think of instructing them in "army" style food preparation strategies. Cleanup procedures for outdoor life have similarities and differences to indoor habits. Campers must now shift to these new strategies. These changes are healthy and break up the camp "routine." It helps prevent "burn out" both for you and your kids.

The kids also learn flexibility—they must learn to adjust to different situations and "roll with the punches" if they feel uncomfortable with their new situation.

Especially refer to The Web (Appendix Figure 1). Consider each box in it for there is much to learn and use from it for this chapter. You know the technique by now. I no longer have to walk you through it.

What about illness "on the road?" Counselors must be aware and vigilant for outdoor and "on the road" injuries and dangers. The more first aid one knows the better! Access to quality medical care must be ensured.

Out under the stars there are dangers. We have animals, plant life and strangers (human) to be concerned with. Always anticipate problems (don't wish for them of course) and be a step ahead of your campers. Teach them good judgment skills for all possible risk situations. Campers must also know, among many other items, how to deal with the bathroom needs that arise in the middle of a dark cold wet evening (or even a warm dry one). You must also reinforce their protective strategies against exposure to the sun, rain, wind, etc.

On camp trips, there are lots of bus rides, train rides or even plane rides. Since most involve buses, good bus safety and behavior techniques must be practiced. How many times have we seen "wild" kids, running and standing on buses, sticking their hands out of the window and/or bothering the driver? What you need to do is sit down by yourself or with colleagues and/or administration and come up with a list of potential problems when it comes to bus safety and procedures. Then organize your list and make a presentation to your group before the trip begins, being certain that everyone understands exactly what is expected and what will happen if rules are not followed. This not only goes for bus safety—it goes for all rules with respect to the trip. The above is exactly how to go about creating, organizing and implementing a policy on anything—here, trip rules in general. First, come to terms with your philosophy on tripping. Second, sit down with a pad and brainstorm ideas on just what you need to involve in your policy or plan. Prioritize your list and organize it. Get further suggestions from colleagues, supervisors, campers, just about anyone who can help you out here. Prepare your notes so that they will become organized into "ready to deliver a speech" form. Gather your campers together and deliver your message. Allow them to ask questions but make sure you remain in control. Be certain that everyone understands your position, philosophy and rules. Also, you must be sure to have an enforcement plan. All of one's policies must contain a well thought-out and "do-able" enforcement plan, without which any policy will be doomed to failure.

So, that comprises the trip chapter. Have a great travel experience!

16

Rainy Days And Mondays Never Get Me Down

In camp, when it rains, things often get very interesting. It becomes a huge challenge to keep procedures running smoothly. Campers are at times confined to their bunks and "cabin fever" can develop. The philosophy is to try and get the kids out of their bunks as much as possible. For example, they can be shuttled to bowling alleys, movie theaters, shows, roller skating rinks and numerous other "under the roof" activities. Some camps have these facilitates on the premises of the camp; for example: "rec" halls, indoor pools etc. When camps have access to these facilities, problems are not as huge.

At times the rain can go on and on—for days—or—the above mentioned facilities may not be available. A lot of creativity is herein obligatory. You can put on talent shows, have "family feuds," "sing-downs," "dating games," "price is rights," etc:—i.e., any of the activities mentioned in Chapters 8 and 12. So we see that there are different types of rainy day philosophies—short term, and long term. With short term strategies, confinement may be for only a few hours. Still, large problems can unfold for these periods of "nothing to do" and "must stay inside these 4 walls." Long term strategies must be implemented for lengthy periods of rain. At times, the strategies overlap.

A few super activities for either need do stand out. One is bingo. Bingo is an activity that is ever-popular. A few items are significant to consider however: First it is essential that "good" prizes are available—i.e., prizes that campers want—wrist bands, head bands, batting gloves, CD's, walkmen, candy, days off at inspection, anything and everything. Find out what it is that your kids would want—and get these items as prizes. Games can be varied, such as full card bingo, X-bingo, 4 corner bingo etc. It is of utmost importance to have a very talented, creative, and funny "caller" for your games, as this keeps interest and motivation "high". If you have things arranged correctly, the game can succeed for as long as a few hours. As mentioned, in one of my previous books, I have some ideas that can be implemented not only for rainy days, but also for rest hours, evening activities, etc. Therefore, from my classroom manual, "Just Let Me Survive Today," let me refer you again to some appropriate excerpts. They are found in the Appendix of this book (in Figures 7 through 10). Please stop and review them again now because they are very appropriate at this juncture.

Bunk members can also get involved with talent shows and many others of the activities mentioned previously.

Another great option for rainy days (and at many other times) is movies, videos, guest speakers, chalk-talks and values-education lessons. The first 2 are self-explanatory. There are some great educational movies and videos out there. Counselors should always consider themselves to be teachers and every moment is another opportunity to teach—through media as here or just through one on one or group discussions to reflect situations occurring on the ball fields, in the bunk, in the dining room, at the activity—anywhere. Remember the philosophy: You are a professional and a teacher! Values education is of utmost import.

Having guest speakers are great ideas. Many camps are able to secure guest speakers like famous athletes or show-biz personalities. These folks can model good sound values for the enthusiastic idol-worshipping kids. Chalk-talks can be valuable rainy (or any) day practices. In them, coaches sit down with groups and go over, via lecture, demonstration or "talk with chalk," good sound techniques for various activities—be they sports, academic, or otherwise. Computer workshops, math seminars, or just about any kind of "chalk-talk" can occur. Yes, this is summer but it can still be a great opportunity for academic "school-like" learning activities. In my second published book called "High-Caliber Kids"—(An Interdisciplinary Book of Values Education)—I have printed over 30 lessons on values education. In the Appendix, in Figures 6 and 12, I include a few sample lessons from this book that can implemented on rainy (or any) days.

One can run indoor tournaments and competitions of all kinds—checkers, chess, indoor soccer, etc. Just remember that these events must be fun, have variations that are "winnable" by possibly anyone (even the seemingly least likely candidate), and they need to be capped off with nice, desirable prizes.

Some times groups may be, with lots of supervision, allowed to engage in activities like "mud sliding" or mud "flag" (touch) football. Weather conditions must not be too severe and the safety of campers must be assured. Use good judgment—never take dangerous risks.

One great activity that worked wonders for me was group trivia contests. Large groups would be gathered in a huge indoor area, like an auditorium, or "boathouse" etc. Teams (usually 6) would be formed and organized in a large circle. Again here, I explain <u>my</u> angle on the game. You must feel free to use your own unique style and creativity to set up your own rules and procedures. Now I continue my presentation to you of "Super-Trivia." The "quiz master" (questioner) comes prepared with questions from show business (movies, songs, TV), current events, sports, camp trivia, just plain wacky questions and questions about anything kids might like and know—riddles, jokes, on and on. For your resources, have at your disposal, TV Guides, Variety Magazine, the newspaper, the internet-anything. Use counselors as scorekeepers, supervisors, etc. I often used a megaphone to call out questions in this large area. When campers know the answer they call it out. Correct responses would generate team points. Wrong answers would result in deductions. Instead of calling out, hand raising might also be employed. Some questions carry bonus points, or be classified "daily doubles" (as on Jeopardy), where point values double. Running scores are announced, and prizes go to winning team members. In case of a "runaway" victory situation, points might also be awarded for 2nd place or even 4th, etc. Just devise methods to keep the interest going even for the last place team. It is best if there is always hope for some sort of victory in all competitions. Spice the event with some Mishigos. Incorporate "steal the bacon" or "beat the clock" activities. That is, for example, each team has its members numbered from 1, to say, 8. Call all #7's to perform some task for time or ask all #7's a question. Bonus points are involved. You get the idea? Teams should all have nicknames—like the "Jets" or the "Superdudes," etc. Teams may be required, for points, to devise team songs, team dances, etc. Have campers volunteer, for points or prizes, to get in the middle of the circle and do a dance or sing a solo. Be creative—have fun! This is a great game with enormous potential for large group interaction.

Then there is our "horse race" activity. This is another super event for rainy (or any) day (or evening). The motif is a racetrack situation. There might be parimutuel windows, ticket sellers, etc. You can get as wild and creative as you chose to. The theme however, is the horse race event. Counselors sit down and choreograph a race: Each "horse" gets "odds" assigned to it and you sit down with paper and pad and diagram the race (who is first at the half-mile pole, the stretch, etc). Select horses with funny names—or use camper's names and modify, like "Billie-Jean Hanover." You then use a tape recorder to record the race as if you were the race announcer. The "call" of the race reflects your choreography or plan. Make it exciting. Make the call "funny"—spice it with humor. Before "post-time" the kids all make bets. They're given play money to wager and are instructed in the methods of betting for this game. Have several races. You might be able to rent videos of real races and dub in your call over the actual race.

There might be entertainment between races. Interview guest celebrities. Allow your creativity to run wild! Winners are those who win the most money. You can also use events like this as springboards for further learning experiences. One, for example, from my book, "High Caliber Kids," is a related values-education (anti-gambling) lesson on "A Day at the Races" Trip which can hopefully be arranged with local racetracks, county fairs or stables. See the Appendix (Figure 13) now for a discussion of this possibility—yet another idea for a fun and learning activity! Also in my book "Just Let Me Survive Today," I outline and elaborate on an academic skills lesson on probability in math by use of this horse race activity. The related excerpt from that text is found on Appendix Figure 9.

To summarize, rainy days can really be rough times. However, with a little creativity and enthusiasm, this potentially disastrous period can be turned around 180 degrees into a wonderful situation. Many of you readers I'm sure have your own unique suggestions for this chapter. Also, as always, you should network with your colleagues, supervisors and even campers to generate further possibilities.

17

An Ounce Of Prevention—A Safety Primer

As camp counselor, we take on the major responsibility of becoming "mom and dad" full-time, big-time, 24-hour a day time. It is great practice, as discussed, for future parental status for the young adult counselor. We become the caretakers, the overseers, of the health and safety of our charges. We must be vigilant for them. There is a long-term or day by day vigilance and then there is short-term or acute care. Let's discuss long-term care initially. These are the every day things that must be attended to. For example, take camper attire.

How many times would my youngsters have gone out in a driving, chilly rainstorm with sneakers, thongs, tee shirts—and no raincoat? The answer is far too many. We must be the guardians of camper dress. We must be sure that they do not overdress as well. In the evening, it must be assured that they are warm enough at bed-time covering them with sufficient blankets as necessary and seeing to it that bunk windows are adjusted appropriately. The children need us here—we must not let them down.

We must be an advocate for their continued (acute care) health throughout the day. In the forest and "woods" there is poison ivy, there are animals, there are other threats. We must respond quickly to insect bites if necessary. We must teach the youngster how to protect themselves from the dangers of exposure to the sun—both for their healthy skin and for aspects relating to potential heatstroke and dehydration. Often, campers develop eye infections (like conjunctivitis), colds, sore throats, GI distress, fever and so on. We must respond to their complaints and always be on the lookout for early symptoms of any distress. Many years ago, one of my best campers (one who hardly ever complained about anything and in addition was a "great kid") suddenly was crying about "pain in my cheeks." We immediately ran him over to the health center (or camp infirmary) where he was promptly diagnosed with mumps and early treatment was initiated. We knew immediately that something was definitely "up" with him.

Sometimes we'll come across the "hypochondriac" kid, who seems to be eternally ill and/or complaining. We must handle this child with understanding and not make fun of his problems. If necessary we may need to consult with camp administrators, child psychologists, and/or the parents of the youngster. Read Chapter 4 for this situation.

At times during our long hard schedule of responsibility, we may run into acute or emergency situations which require even quicker responses. It would help greatly if the counselor was trained in some sort of first aid—the more the better. Always try to get the victim stabilized and comfortable but never violate basic first aid cautions—i.e., don't move a suspected victim of spinal cord injury if at all possible, etc. In any event—stay calm and get rid of "gawkers" and "rubbernecking" curiosity seekers. Try to calm the victim. Hopefully your camp will conduct at least some orientation into techniques of emergency care. At some point—as early as possible—make contact with experts who can deal directly with the problem. If at camp contact your supervisors immediately. If off camp contact necessary medical personnel and also contact your supervisors back at camp as soon as you can. Use good common sense and sound judgment. Sometimes, lives can be saved!

Also, as far as strangers go: When away from camp of course teach them to steer clear of any strangers and to report any immediately! If at an off-camp movie, e.g., be sure that counselors never lose sight of the kids, even escorting them to the bathroom as necessary to maintain vigilance.

Let's further discuss the importance of safety skills throughout your <u>entire</u> day. When you're on the ball fields you're making sure that no bats are in use when campers are standing too close. At sports activities, you're further watching that: a) catchers are wearing masks; b) equipment is in proper working order; c) golf clubs are being swung safely; d) bats are not left on the ground where folks can trip over them; e) soccer matches do not get out of control; f) hockey sticks are not swung over a certain height; g) good, safe gymnastics safety is practiced; and h) protection from sun problems are always implemented. The list goes on and as you read, add your own points as well.

In the bunks you're watching for a) shower-time safety; b) controlling excess "horseplay"; and c) preventing verbal arguments from escalating into physical confrontations. At arts and crafts you're watching for safe "shop" techniques with machine safety being practiced. At the waterfront, your eyes and ears are always on full-scale alert because mistakes there often do not ever get corrected. Watch everywhere for electrical wires hanging down from old constructions. Be ever watchful!

To summarize, you must help teach your campers how to be safe and healthy. You must be their eyes and ears until they learn to use their own effectively. You must protect them—you must not let them down! They need you!

In many of the previous chapters, we have discussed safety aspects in even greater detail. Always be sure safety is one of the prime considerations in everything that you do.

18

A Friend Indeed (Camp Friendships Are Forever)

The purpose of this brief chapter is to express another huge benefit derived from the camping experience. Throughout my 25 years of camping, I had the opportunity to make many close friends as well as loads of contacts. Because of the close, day to day, 24 hour, often continuous sharing of experiences, the chance of forming very close friendships (often lasting for my lifetime), are present. In fact most of my very best relationships have come out of my camping experience. I've learned about friendship, caring, helping, teamwork, responsibility, manners, self-reliance, self-esteem and loads of other essential qualities and values. I've stayed in touch with some of my friends over my lifetime. Contacts made in camp can carry over into your personal and business lives. The memories of camp life will be forever etched in the psyches of all who have even just a brief taste of the camping experience.

It would behoove staff to take advantage of the extreme power inherent in the camping world to foster some of these ideas, feelings and values in the campers. Encourage these bonds that will result in life-enhancing relationships. Promote socialization and the learning of high caliber values.

19

Values For The Games People Play (For The Athlete In The Crowd)

Of course in camp there are many opportunities for sporting events. This chapter gives a general review of the athletics program, especially from the standpoint of Values Education.

For the most part, the goal of camp athletics is pure fun and enjoyment on the part of the camper. There are however, lots of fringe benefits as well. Campers have the opportunity to learn of sportsmanship, teamwork, fair play and integrity. Their physical skills become enhanced; their self-confidence can often be elevated. They get to experience the thrill of victory and learn how to handle the "agony of defeat."

Counselors at all levels have the enviable opportunity of teaching much of the above to their charges. At many athletic areas there will be specialists for each individual activity. For example, when the kids get to the basketball court there will be a specialist there to inculcate those unique skills of this net game. The campers don't just play; they learn skills and techniques by performing drills and receiving "chalk talks" by the experts.

As mentioned, there is a great opportunity for values education here on the fields as well. How many times have I witnessed children saying to teammates, "You stink—you made us lose," or "You're chucked!" (in NYC in the 50's and 60's this meant you're out of the game). I've witnessed campers throwing their gloves at teammates in softball and the very ball itself at teammates in basketball. There are horrible occurrences of this nature—and worse—that go on with kids. What about the incident in September '96 of Robby Alomar of the Orioles spitting on an ump! What a negative role model he was! Or the infamous "head–butt" in the 2006 World Cup!! So, here is where we have the golden opportunity to teach that this type of behavior is simply unacceptable and will not be tolerated. We can do it by using one on one discussions, group lectures, sanctions, punishments, and by having pro-athletes and other potential role models come in and speak about it.

I would like to share one very interesting philosophy that the director of my summer camp had. He would not allow for the "choosing of sides" for teams—as was traditionally done in NYC and, as I would guess, almost everywhere else kids played ball. His belief was that the kids chosen toward the end would be very hurt by the frequent humiliation—especially since many "choosers" were often overheard to say things like: "He stinks, I don't want him—no way—you take him!". Well, our director wanted to protect the camper from this sort of treatment! Therefore, his rule, which was never to be broken, was to have the supervising counselor on the scene "make sides"—i.e., make the teams himself. This way, no one would be embarrassed and made to feel very low. In addition, team composition could be quite evenly matched. I totally agreed with this unique notion and thought it to be quite meaningful. Many on staff thought it to be unrealistic—believing that "life is hard and these kids have got to get used to or at least learn to deal with rejection, put downs and ridicule." I don't agree! WE can run our schools, our classrooms, our camps, our playgrounds as we would want the world to be, yet still teach coping skills for life's harsh realities. So, on the ball fields and at the activity areas, let's all have fun, but always capitalize on our golden opportunities to teach values.

In other words, we can use the teaching methods inherent in The Web. Start by brainstorming all the various values and attitudes that you would like your kids to acquire. Write them all down. Use one on one talks as well as group discussion to begin changing viewpoints. Employ some of the lessons (or similar ones) appearing in my book "High Caliber Kids" (see, for example, the Appendix, Figures 5, 6, 11, and 12). These lessons are "ready to go" anytime—at evening activity, rest period, etc., and they can involve values learning via role-play, dramatic presentation and trips, among other methods. Of course it would be great if you could enlist the help of role models from the field of sports or even from the camp itself. Experience will certainly help you to teach your lessons better and better down through the years. As usual, patience and perseverance are essential ingredients for our kids who are just beginning, in many cases, to learn about getting along with teammates. The media, i.e., via movies, videos, TV, songs, etc., can help enormously here. There are many great pieces out there that teach values in a glitzy "show bizzy" type way that can effectively motivate the campers to really want to "do the right thing." At any moment you may need to "seize the opportunity" and become an "on the spot" values educator, i.e., when for example, that budding Robby Alomar/John McEnroe clone (of the 90's) does his (or her) unsportsmanlike thing (or when the 2005 Pistons/Pacers "into the stands" debacle–type situation arises). You call a total timeout, gather your troops together and do your values education work. The moment may come up at <u>any</u> time—seize it, use it! You may have your own great ideas on how to teach values (especially here on the ball fields)—if so, use your creativity in this critical area! If you seem to be up against some really resistant and difficult kids here, there is always Chapter 4 to consult. First you do need a philosophy here. For me, this topic is numero uno. In fact, I would like you to re-read my philosophy of education, which is found in Chapter 2. After you establish your own personal philosophy on values and how you want them taught, it becomes time to network and brainstorm in order to start putting together an outline of your methodology. As always, a little "Shtick and Mishigos" cannot hurt. It may provide uniquely motivational examples to get even the most resistant participant going. Let your creative juices flow here. For example, in hockey, there is a "Lady Byng Trophy" awarded to the player with the best sportsmanship. In beauty pageants there is a "Miss Congeniality." Create your own awards for sportsmanship and values and make them just as important as the regular MVP trophy. Promote these awards to a large degree. This is just one example of a piece of public relations that can be employed. Have a "Lady Byng" All-Star Game, etc.

20

Let's Go Visiting: (Tips For Visiting Day)

Visiting Day is an extremely important one. Campers are anxiously awaiting the sights and sounds of their parents. Parents can't wait to see their most precious possessions once again! Camp staff wants to make a good impression. Everyone is on their "best behavior."

What are the "purposes and goals" of visiting day? Parents want to see the camp, its facilities, and, of course, as stated, their children. Kids want to see their parents—both groups miss one another tremendously. Parents want to talk to staff about the progress of their children and the staff often desires to communicate with the parents—about both positive and negative issues.

The "camp" (all its employees and administrators), wants to "look good." Most camps will naturally make it a priority to look even better than usual at this time. And this is only natural. When one has guests coming over, most will make it a priority to "clean house" 110%. "Camps" naturally desire for a good impression too. This is good, smart, public relations.

Parents are going to ask counselors how their child is doing. Whenever there are problems, it is always wise to be as diplomatic as possible. You need to express yourself but also must guard against being too negative. Sandwich your complaints between "let's work together on the problem," and your son has "lots of potential." This is not phony talk—it is simply a way to get your point across in a positive format. As a teacher, I often need to deal with "open-school" days. In my book, "Just Let Me Survive Today," I touch on techniques of parental contact on the phone and in person. Let me give you an excerpt from that book that is appropriate to this topic: It can be found in Appendix Figure 14.

Always stress that you and the parents are part of the problem-solving team and are to work with the same great teamwork exhibited by any successful team.

The Camp Director usually has an extremely busy day—hearing about alleged counselor verbal and/or physical abuse to complaints about everything from the camp food to the camp doctor. If you've been doing an honest professional job with high moral integrity then most likely your name will not be heard in negative administrator-parent conferences. Always take the high road with your camp kids—treat them with respect and courtesy and likely they'll reciprocate. Follow all the teachings of this manual and you'll be extremely successful!

What to be vigilant for on visiting day and shortly thereafter: Major bouts of homesickness directly following parental visits—understandable for sure! Just dust off your PhD in psychology and take out your supply of extra patience and understanding. The kids may require extra long talks in the evening, at rest hour, or as needed. Just be there for your kids—now and always; some parents, despite camp warnings, insist on buying and bringing up loads of candy and other food. It seems at times like Halloween (after trick or treat) to the 3rd power. This quantity of food is not only unhealthy for the camper, but also is a sanitation nightmare. So be sure your camp has policies on food confiscation and enforce them strictly.

Most good camps, in fact, have a huge visiting day orientation for staff replete with meetings, conferences, Q&A sessions, guest speakers, role play situations and lots of staff development activities. In fact, most good camps have similar arrangements for almost all special events and activities.

So let us now summarize some important bits about visiting day by examining our Web. First, the general counselor starts out with his (or her) philosophy (a subset of the camp philosophy) on the day itself. What are your goals? What do you want to accomplish? The camp's philosophy, as usual, should be a major component of your own philosophy. Then it is brainstorming time. Make a list of important points to consider on visiting day. Record them and organize them. Get set to implement them. Do a "walk through" in your mind of a typical visiting day scenario. Get all the staff development that you can accumulate on this important day. Do it via group meetings and one on one sessions with experienced colleagues. Also campers must know exactly what is in store for them on visiting day. You must issue them an enforceable and reasonable set of rules—regarding candy e.g., and all other procedures. Have discussions with your kids, via one-on-ones and group meetings regarding the various aspects of the parental (reuniting) meeting and then the eventual separation. Talk with them about homesickness and their feelings regarding visiting day. Of course, do it all on their appropriate age level and need. Have role models come in and address them on reuniting and separations. There is much in the way of values education that can be implemented here. From the media, TV shows and videos are available on issues that the kids are about to face. Have them role play and discuss their feelings. There is a great need, during this, possibly very stressful time for them, for you to spend quality time with your kids. Seize those "minute by minute" teaching opportunities that can arise regarding visiting day, both before and after. Always deal with your kids, as usual, in your very sensitive manner, understanding what they must be going through in seeing their parents after such a long absence. This period will require patience and perseverance by you. Also, accounts of experiences on this issue, which you can elicit from fellow staff, will help you to deal more effectively with visiting day. As usual, when you think you are lost, read Chapter 4 and use it to guide you. Ensure the safety of your kids. Be aware that, in extreme cases, after visiting day, campers can have thoughts of "running away" or might become very depressed. Always consider the possibilities and have strategies for dealing with them. The need for Shtick and Mishigos here is not so great since the extreme excitement generated by the day itself provides quite enough enthusiasm. Keep in mind that for some, there are other problems that you must deal with by using these same methods: children of divorced and separated parents; children of families with a parent missing because of death; children whose parents just do not visit—for a myriad of reasons. So the brainstorming we spoke of earlier must reach out to kid <u>issues</u> as well.

Back to your own staff development for a moment. Attend (and be very attentive at) all meetings and sessions regarding this day. Be patient as you learn and try to absorb knowledge from the experienced colleagues and supervisors with whom you will network! Of course throughout the entire time, your own creative thoughts should be evident. So we see again, that visiting day (and most camp days) is not as simple and straightforward as it might at first appear. This day, as every other one, in order to be magnificently successful (and there's no reason for you to accept any less) will require a lot of hard work and effort! There is a lot at stake though. I've seen a few kids "lost" at visiting day. By this I mean for example, that they get so homesick and agitated that they wind up either going home soon thereafter, or they are really "messed up" in this regard for the rest of the season—certainly not returning the following summer.

So don't take this day lightly. Some campers will breeze through it with no problem at all. But for some, it is critical that <u>you</u> be there in mind, body and spirit to provide the support that they may need. I know you can and will succeed here. You must!

21

You Are How You Eat—Manners And The Dining Room Experience

Campers spend a great deal of time in the dining room and this fact thus provides us with another golden opportunity to teach more of those good values. As a professional, you should take advantage of this chance to mold the habits of your campers effectively and to send them home with impressive manners as well as positive attitudes with regard to the dining experience—another feather in their caps of growing up properly and admirably. It may come as no surprise to the staffer that campers often are not well-schooled in proper "eating etiquette." Many have never learned correctly at home and hence your table will become the classroom. Your teaching methods can vary. You can teach good manners as you go along, meal by meal. You can take your "class" down to the dining area as a "dry run" practice activity during "non-eating" hours. You can conduct lectures, have rap-groups and workshops, have "guest" lecturers, and take field trips to restaurants to practice on these new skills. You may give awards and prizes to motivate and teach and get really creative with this concept—even as far as conducting "Manners Olympics" and "World Cup or Super Bowl of Manners Competitions."

As far as content goes—what kind of manners should you teach? Well, first of course, you must develop a philosophy of your own on this topic. Also, you must create your own ideal techniques that you will teach to your kids. One to one tutoring for "problem" kids may be necessary. What about this subject matter?

Well, you can include, amongst other possibilities: using important words, like please and thank you; techniques of sharing; portion sizes; how to hold your utensils properly; preventing food fights; how to sit properly when in the dining room; how to pass up, clean up, stack waiter trays, scrape plates, and much much more. Many camps have varied religious programs that include additional activities at mealtime.

The key to all is mutual respect and adherence to a set of rules and regulations for dining behavior. So again, here is yet another chance to inculcate some excellent values so that the children emerge "better" (citizens) for having been associated with your leadership abilities!

22

Prizes And Awards—Incentives To Motivate

Prizes. We have not mentioned that much about this topic. A big motivation for students (in school) is grades. In addition, however, I offer my students in school rewards and prizes to help motivate them. In camp this practice is extremely effective. What are the prizes awarded? They can be virtually anything, but most popular are: head bands, wrist bands, batting gloves, trophies and certificates at ceremonies and banquets, cassette tapes, VCR tapes, athletic equipment, extra desserts, free snacks, extra privileges, free days-off at inspection, special meals with VIP's and any number of other items.

The point is, offer prizes and rewards as motivators. They work! Find out what it is that your individual kids would want and get these items. What do they win prizes for? Anything and everything—trivia and bingo contests, family feuds, athletic prowess, league leadership, MVP status, and much more. Since I have used the "prize technique" so effectively in the school setting (in fact I received a grant from the NYC Board of Education for its implementation), I include, in the Appendix, Figure 15, an excerpt from my "Survive" book on prize philosophy in the classroom. Again, simply extrapolate to summer camp.

23

Primarily Pranks (Know 'Em All)

Throughout the book, I have referred occasionally to "pranks." These are little acts of "terror" that campers do to counselors and to each other, and that counselors do to campers and to each other. For the most part, I don't like them and disapprove of them. Some camps have pranks as traditional components of the program. Most of them, although intended for fun ("good, clean fun"), usually wind up hurting someone, either physically or emotionally. Some might be grounds for dismissal and even of corporal punishment (criminal) charges. They are not fun and should be avoided. Some pranks, among the hundreds, to watch for are: dumping of water on counselors via elaborate hook-ups by the doors of the bunks, counselors tickling the noses of sleeping campers after loading their scratching hands with shaving cream; counselors waking up campers in the middle of the night with pizza treats spiked with "hot" sauce; staff leading half-asleep campers on a "night walk" or requiring campers to do rigorous physical activities while in their pajamas—liking holding a pair of sneakers at arms length as "punishment" for some action during the day; placing beds in weird locations so that campers or counselors, upon waking, are totally confused about their whereabouts; going on "raids" to other bunks—especially those containing members of the opposite sex; "short-sheeting" beds so that the individual's feet smack against the shorted sheet upon trying to get into the bed; loading beds up with annoying "stuff"—like food, insects, animals and worse.

You can't believe these things actually do take place? They do and must be forbidden. They are mostly abusive and again, may often be grounds for immediate expulsion from camp for those responsible. Consult with all aspects of The Web in order to repel these actions—by making it clear through all available methods, that this kind of activity is absolutely unacceptable.

24

In The Heat of the Night—(O.D.'s Beware)

One of the most crucial times for the camp counselor (and for the camp itself) is the evening, after evening activity has ended. Many camps have a bugle that sounds "Taps," to signify the peaceful end to the busy day. However, for many campers, "Taps" is really the signal to "Let's get goin' here, have a ball and see if we can in any way tease and torture the "O.D." (the sad sack who's "on duty" for the evening). As veteran staff would know that it is because of the potential for nocturnal disaster, that this chapter takes on such import.

Hold the disaster! In fact, just the opposite can be attained by the shrewd and clever staffer. This evening time can be a wonderful opportunity for staff and children to get much "closer" with one another, and thus to relate on a more intimate level. The groundwork for this situation is put down the very first night of camp—when most campers are a bit tense and many might be unfamiliar with new faces. This first evening provides a chance to establish some security and to lay down some of "your rules." On this first evening, when the lights are out, run through some of your very basic rules and philosophies and talk about what you expect from the campers—especially in the area of behavior. Be friendly but firm. You'll go through all (or most) of your rules the following (first) day. Let the campers know that you will not tolerate any major nonsense at night. What kind of nonsense are we talking about? Well, campers often, among other things already mentioned, have water fights, raids to other bunks, fights (pillow, wrestling matches, boxing matches), bully some of the "weaker" members of the bunk and abuse the O.D.—via numerous creative techniques—too numerous to mention, and growing every summer. We want to prevent (both psychological and physical) injury to our campers and staff. There are ways to have a good time without anyone getting hurt.

Possibly during the first night, but definitely at times during the rest of the season, this is a wonderful opportunity (as is rest hour) for a "Good and Welfare." It is when you go around the bunk and each member has a chance to speak his (or her) mind. It is a great exercise in human relations for all. However, certain ground rules must be observed. For example, most comments should include those of the positive, constructive variety. If anything negative is said, it must be done so with utmost tact and sensitivity to the feelings of all concerned. Once you speak and have your say, you may not speak again. The purpose of these discussions is to allow the youngsters to express their thoughts and feelings in a constructive, positive way—a skill that will become an even greater asset to them later in life. A menu of constructive activities for after dark should be suggested: for example, quiet reading and/or discussions; listening to a transistor radio or walkman with earplugs; let your and their creativity be your guide! One summer I did observe some counselors organizing planned, supervised, pillow fights. I do not usually approve of <u>any</u> kind of horseplay, but the particular staff member had it organized very safely and to every minute detail. The probability for injury was very slim; no one got hurt and the kids really enjoyed it. The point is, if <u>any</u> horseplay at all is involved, it must be <u>very carefully</u> supervised. What to do if your rules are violated? Well, we have the all-purpose rule-enforcement chapter (Chapter 3) that is essential to understand.

Good evening discipline is very important to attain because without it, injuries can occur and campers might be extremely tired the following day. However, one can not just simply "snap" ones fingers and expect good nighttime behavior to result. It will take careful planning, creative thinking, hard work and desire. Look to another tour of the Web for further solutions here. By this, of course, I mean you're consulting and considering all Web components as we've done so many times already.

25

Bunk Inspection Primer

What about some more of the basics of inspection? As we have mentioned, it is quite important that bunks be kept in a relatively neat state for at least the majority of the day. If this is not enforced, very quickly your bunk will turn into an ugly mess and a hazard to the health of all. To set the tone, it is advisable to have a rigorous morning inspection followed by more cursory checks later in the day. Clean-up should begin promptly upon dismissal from breakfast. A "work-wheel" or (similar) rotating chart of assignments is posted in the bunk. Each camper is responsible for a certain job on a daily revolving basis. For example, some jobs might be: sweep the bunk; clean the bathroom area; straighten the drawers and cubbies; clean the outside grounds; sweep the porch; empty the garbage; hold the dustpan; day off; bunk captain; fix the shoe racks; etc. Campers do each job, ideally, carefully and effectively. Jobs have certain specific guidelines, creatively outlined by staff: "Cubby-fixers," e.g., need only inform (and briefly help) those with messy cubbies to straighten them out.

Then, at about 9:15 AM, the "Inspector," (usually the groupleader of another group—or your own), comes down and performs his examination. Ten point zero for a "perfect" bunk and tenth-of-a-point deductions for each deficiency. For example, a 9.5 is given to a bunk with approximately five deductions. Bunks compete against one another and weekly winners are declared—with prizes (like free canteen or ice cream) awarded to the most outstanding bunks.

It sounds pretty simple and straight-forward. Yeah! Like a two year old going to bed without any problem. There usually <u>are</u> problems—like fighting between bunkmates, yelling and put-downs; some campers being very lazy and uncooperative, etc. What to do? As usual, consult The Web. Turn to page Appendix Figure 1 and examine The Web. Inspection can really make or break a day in many ways. Not only might you lose control of the neatness of your bunk, but you may very well lose the co-operation of your kids as well. This is a very important activity, this inspection. First we brainstorm with co-counselors, veteran staff members, administrators, etc. We establish a philosophy of inspection first. Just what do we want from our kids in the way of work here? What kind of responsibility and habits of cleanliness do we want to create? Our philosophy is shaped not only by our own ideas (formulated in conjunction with our discussions with colleagues and administrators), but, as we said, is going to be in sync with camp philosophy on this topic as well.

Our brainstorming leads us to the development of the work rotation schedule, along with its various job assignments. Via group discussion at various times during the day, as well as one on one raps as needed, campers gradually grasp the idea behind inspection as well as your expectations regarding it. Values education lessons on cleanliness and habits thereof, are essential. Role models in the camp community might be called on to illustrate healthy techniques in the area of cleanup. The media can be used to further the attaining of the feel for the importance of clean-up. Also, victorious bunks (in inspection) are lauded, awarded and publicized. Remember too, that, as always, your rules (your jobs and expectations) must be reasonable and enforceable. Seize those golden teaching opportunities that will likely arise quite often in this situation. In other words, if there is some sort of "breakdown" at inspection time, work on the problem right at that moment or make a note of it and be sure to work on it later (after perhaps jotting down some important strategies you plan on using to deal with on the problem). Quality time with your bunk must be spent by you during cleanup time. You must help out and supervise and not run to your bed (as some do) for a quick morning siesta while things completely deteriorate around you. You will lose your kids and deserve the bad vibes you will get. If you are stuck and don't know how to proceed further—consult Chapter 4 for some possible assistance. Throughout the inspection process put your own creativity to work. Come up with new and unique angles that may change or modify the inspection situation.

As far as safety: Be sure that inspection time is a safe time and that constant supervision is in place. Shtick and Mishigos activities and ideas can serve to stimulate the interbunk competition that might be necessary to maintain the good motivation needed to spur campers on to an effective cleanup situation. For example: Have a camper inspect every so often; have Elvis or Michael (Jordan or Jackson) come to inspect; put on a show about inspection or; employ any other unique idea to effect success in this area of motivation.

Some camps out there may not have a rigorous inspection or may have none at all for that matter. This is a mistake. Again, it is quite important to have clean bunks, as well as to train campers in responsible living.

To work on any significant problem relating to inspection, role play situations can be developed and used as an evening activity, rest hour exercise, camp play, etc. This issue gives to the sort of creative problem solving, discussed here. You might spend some time on an inspection issue, e.g., instead of a scheduled activity, if the situation is serious enough. You can use a "walk-through" (dry-run) inspection to recreate and work on an inspection related problem that seems resistant to traditional problem—solving techniques. Similar though somewhat unrelated to this would be a walk—through regarding the dining room. For example, say camper manners have been (or have become) extremely deficient. Then you can perhaps, instead of say, a period 5 activity, spend the time lining up and proceeding to the dining area for a walk-through and rap session with your bunk based on effective table manner strategies.

Back to inspection though! Remember, it is a very important time and must not be ignored. Use common sense and The Web to devise an effective teaching program for inspection.

One mention of two of our jobs: captain and day off. The captain for a day simply acts as a (benevolent) supervisor, facilitator, and chief consultant to the bunk for the cleanup process. He helps everyone out, offers advice, but is not there to yell at folks who are not doing the right thing. The captain reports lazy and ineffective workers to the counselor for follow-up.

Another job is that of "day off." It is basically self-explanatory. Some really generous kids do "volunteer work" on their day off.

Counselors, good luck with this very challenging task!

26

Putting It All Together

Well I hope you enjoyed this manual. Used effectively, I believe that the power and wisdom (based on experience) contained in its pages will help to make your summer enjoyable, and richly rewarding. It will help you to reach out, touch and improve the entire lives of so many more campers than you would have ever imagined possible. If they can ever find you in their later lives they will be unable to ever thank you enough. They and you will realize the impact and significance of your contribution to their lives, the camp, and society as a whole. You are communicating values and ideals that will help make the world a better place in which to live. You are learning and then teaching parenting and human relations skills that are invaluable.

Appendix

FIGURE 1: THE WEB OF SOLUTIONS

The Web

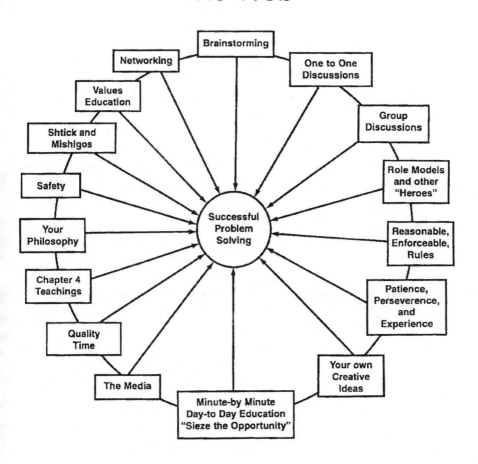

FIGURE 2: RULES IN THE CLASSROOM

As a first year teacher, I had a great number of problems with my classroom management skills. There was often chaos in the class and I frequently went home quite upset and dejected. However, little by little, I learned. Experience was a great teacher. In my second year of teaching, as mentioned previously, I came across a veteran Dean who had a reputation for being strict and "mean." I also mentioned that she spent a great deal of time with me explaining some of her techniques. The big item was her creation and distribution of a set of class rules early in the term. I liked this idea. It gave the children a structure, a framework, a model, to follow. I, however, wanted to be fair, firm, and reasonable—not "mean." So I created a set of rules that I could live with—that felt right for me. This is what you must do. You should create a set of rules that suits your personality—rules that you feel you can enforce and that are well worth enforcing.

The time that the rules should be introduced is at the very beginning of the term. It might take a few days or even a week to get through them. You can review some each day. However, it is essential that the pupils know exactly what is expected of them by you. These rules are the core of classroom management.

In figure 37 (appendix of "Survive" book) appear the complete set of my class rules. They should serve as a guide for you. Remember, be yourself! Your rules can be similar to mine, much less elaborate, or not even printed up at all. If you do make copies of the rules for all of your pupils, give them out the first week of school. Go over them in complete detail as soon as possible. Have them sign the stub as a kind of contractual agreement.

I am now going to go over the rules in detail. Adjust for yourself as necessary. The rules are divided into two basic sections. First there are the essential rules themselves. Section two deals with enforcement procedures. Adjustments to the basic rules can be made during the year from time to time as needed.

FIGURE 3: DISCIPLINE WITH DIGNITY EXCERPT

Pupils and parents must always be treated fairly, legally, ethically, and with respect and dignity. They must never be "put down" or made to feel inferior. As a Dean I especially saw the importance of these actions and feelings. Each case or situation is unique and must be dealt with on an individual basis. There often may be a need for great creativity on your part. When I was Dean, students frequently wanted to speak to me when they were having difficulties: "I want to speak to Mr. Richman—only him," was often heard in the halls of my J.H.S...Why? In addition to all the reasons previously discussed, there was another. I always listened to both sides of every story before making any decisions. Especially note the words "I always listened." Also, I knew my pupils well. In most cases I knew their school histories. I knew what made them get angry and what made them happy. I had knowledge of their home situations and often had met or spoken to their parents. Slowly you get to know your pupils and this of course helps you to deal more effectively with their problems.

In addition to talking to them and their parents, there are also numerous other sources of information at school that can and should be tapped. There are your teaching colleagues who could add new insights into your dealings with individual pupils. There is the guidance department, where the staff, as well as information found in cumulative records, could provide useful information about your children. The school Dean or disciplinarian may have dealt with the pupil previously and may have available useful data. In New York City we have an "SBST (School Based Support) Team" composed of a social worker, a psychologist and an educational evaluator. These folks are extremely important in building your tree of knowledge about a student. Anyone and everyone in the school might be useful as sources of information—security guards, lunchroom staff, administrators, other pupils, etc. However, student confidentiality must always be protected. In using all these people on a daily basis and in networking with them you get to "hear things" through the school "grapevine,"—that all important informal network that exists in all schools and organizations.

So as far as gathering information, we see that there are a huge number of sources of our key "data" about a given pupil. Now once we have this information, what do we do with it? Each case is completely unique. Let's take an example. A pupil is misbehaving in class—constantly chattering with the person sitting next to him. I ask him to please relocate himself to another seat (I tell him exactly where) in the room. He absolutely refuses insisting that he "didn't do anything"…"why should I move?" In order to prevent a confrontation, I allow him to remain in his seat…for now.

After class, I quickly check with some of my "sources." I find that Johnny often responds to one on one conferences with the teacher and that phone calls and parental involvement often, in the past, have proven to be of little help. Great! This is my first method of choice anyway. We sit and talk and together we pick out a more comfortable seat for the youngster. Also, the reasons behind my original request to him, as well as his need to obey, are discussed. Perhaps my "sources" might have pointed to some other initial step.

When there is a problem, make a plan of action. Gather information. Investigate. Then consult with others and decide what to do. Make the decision. Sometimes your method of dealing with a problem will be right and will be successful. At other times it will fail. However, you will learn, and gradually—often quickly, your techniques will improve.

Once in my early years of teaching some possession of mine "disappeared" from my desk. My first thought was that a pupil definitely stole it. I looked around for it and it was nowhere to be found. I announced to the class that "An item was stolen from my desk and it must be returned immediately." Of course, five minutes later it either turned up under a pile of papers or I realized that I had left it home. From that moment on I decided never to "jump to conclusions" without investigating a situation first. As Dean I often received discipline referrals from teachers accusing students of various levels of misbehavior. At times, upon investigation, I found that the accusations were either false, greatly exaggerated or totally the result of inappropriate teacher behavior. Again the point is—always listen to all sides of a story—investigate, network, consult—and then make your decision.

There will be times when you may need to refer situations to the Dean or Assistant Principal. However, often you will solve problems on your own and the more experienced and successful you become the fewer problems you will have. Speak to students privately and not in front of their peers. Their attitudes will always be more positive and the results much more successful. Talk to your students. Listen to what they have to say. Be fair and honest with them. Get to know them! Treat them with respect and dignity.

These crucial one-on-one teacher-pupil meetings usually cannot be held during your class period. After class is over or on one of your free or prep periods, find out where the student is, and go to that location. Ask permission from the teacher of that class and take the pupil into the hall or into a school office where there are people around but where you still will be able to talk confidentially. At times I have called the pupil's home and instead of speaking to the parent, I ask to speak to the pupil. Or, I've written letters expressing my feelings to the pupil directly. However, the far and away best procedure is to have those one-on-one, face to face, private conferences, where you try to work things out in a very non-confrontational way. Also, by attending informal school events such as athletic contests, dances, plays etc., I am able to establish better relationships with my students. Either assigned or unassigned, I've often gone into the lunchroom or into gym classes to mingle with pupils on an informal basis. Get involved in school activities as much as you can!

FIGURE 4: CLASSROOM ENFORCEMENT
TECHNIQUES

Next comes the critical area of rule violation and enforcement procedures. Without a viable enforcement system, the rules are meaningless and the entire package of rules will be useless. At this point I discuss with the class a basketball game, explaining that if there were no rules, players would be jumping on one another's backs and punching each other to prevent scoring. Without traffic rules cars would be smashing into one another all over town, going through red lights and driving at dangerous speeds. I develop this idea for my class rules as well. I inform the children that living by the rules will usually result in excellent grades and "may" result in a "good" phone call home. I at times use words like "may" rather than "will" because the former does not lock you in to an act as does the latter. Always praise and reward positive acts. If violations do occur, any number of sanctions or combinations thereof might occur. In my "official rules," (figure 37 in the actual "Survive book), I label them from A through I.

First let us look at Section A. I keep an anecdotal record of rule violations, as elaborate as is needed, depending on the class. With some classes it takes the form of "zeros." A zero is given for talking, calling out, coming late without a pass, being unprepared, etc. A zero lowers the grade by one point each. A record is kept in this area. To have a zero removed a pupil must exhibit excellent behavior for 2 full days. So, they come very quickly but take a while to disappear. Every so often I inform pupils of their "zero status." They look forward to this "zero report" and are proud when they have none or have worked them all off. This zero idea works extremely well with many classes and might be all the disciplining that is required. However some pupils may not care all that much about the "zero count." For these pupils we must proceed further. Also, every so often I have a "good and welfare" session whereby we go around the room and each pupil has 30 seconds or so to comment on any aspect of class. They are free to say anything within reason and must present criticism tactfully and with positive intent. Once they speak they cannot comment again. They can pass if they want to and I am the final speaker here. Of course it must be done carefully and the ground rules must be clearly understood by all. However, it can be extremely positive for pupil and class morale.

When a pupil does not respond to the zero procedure, we often resort to option B on our list. Option B involves a "warning" conference by me. I ask the pupil to remain after class or seek him or her out later in the day during one of my free periods. I sit him down away from friends and "peer pressure" and try to just get to the bottom of the problem. I try to work it out before it gets any more serious. I attempt to reason with the pupil and hope to establish a positive relationship. As an alternative method, I have even called home and asked to speak to the pupil and not to the parent. However, it is best to deal with it in school on that one to one, face to face, human relations oriented basis. It can work beautifully. I also inform the pupil what I must do if the problem continues. I thus warn him.

Part C again involves the section sheet/conduct book idea that is of use in some schools.

Then comes step D—the parental letter or phone call. I have stopped with letters and now always opt for phone calls. It's far more personal, allows for a give and take, and is always more effective. Only when steps A through C are not successful need I resort to step D. As I have gained more and more experience down through the years, I have found that most behavioral issues can be terminated successfully at step B. Let's stop here for a minute to talk about the all important phone call.

I often advise new teachers or teachers having difficulty to use the phone more often. They often come back with: "I made twenty calls last night and the kids are still out of control—worse than ever." The phone is not a magical and mystical device that instantly halts disruptive behavior in children. It is only one ingredient in an entire arsenal of techniques. Also, to use it successfully requires practice and care. Its effective use is an art. When you speak to parents, always be courteous and respectful. Have a positive opening line and end on an upbeat note as well. In the middle somewhere strategically and tactfully place what is on your mind. Stress that both of you comprise a team that is working cooperatively with pupil success as your common, ultimate aim. The technique takes lots of practice. Eventually you will see the positive results of its power. Your pupils will see it and their parents will see it as well. You will learn how to deal with a variety of situations that might arise—the pupil himself answers the phone, the parent is not home, big brother answers, etc. You will learn which time of the day is the best—usually the evening. Who is the "better" contact—the mother or father? Often other teachers, guidance counselors or administrators may give you pointers in dealing with certain individual pupils. You always should consult with them if you have any questions. There is much to learn, much to experience and much to gain. In less than one percent of the time have I had negative experiences in this area. However, you must learn what to do in these situations—that is, if a parent gets hostile, etc. Usually you just end the conversation politely and consult with administration or guidance the next day. As with most everything else, trial and error and inquiry are the best teachers here. When I first began teaching back in the early seventies, the course instructor of our "rookie teacher rap group" held up a telephone and said that it would be a powerful tool in classroom management. He was correct.

When we must resort to steps E, F and G, we have a serious problem on our hands. Because of my vast experience, it is now very rare if this point is reached, but it was much more often, earlier in my career. There does come a time when you have done everything humanly possible—you've had private conferences with the pupil, tried zeros, spoke with the parent, etc., and still you have trouble. Now you need some extra help. Your school should have an AP or Dean who steps in now to provide you with assistance. The pupil should be referred to this specialist at this point along with an anecdotal record of pupil infractions, plus all the steps you have taken to try to solve the problem. Assuming you've done most everything possible, dealt with all involved in a respectful and constructive way, it now becomes the role of the person on the next higher rung on the "ladder of discipline" to help. This person characteristically will speak to the pupil first. Then, if needed, she will speak to the parent on the phone and very often will invite the parent up for a conference with you, her (the dean or A.P.), the pupil, or any combination thereof. Next, step H involves documented "pre-suspension" or guidance conferences and at times suspension might eventually result. Many schools have various programs seeking alternatives to suspense. At times it becomes clear that nothing is going to work. At this point it becomes necessary to involve guidance, social services and/or counseling. Possible placement in an alternative program may be an option in your school. Of course, guidance and counseling may be incorporated much earlier on in this process as well. When the top rung of the ladder of discipline is reached, a jump-off option into a completely different kind of program may be appropriate. However, most problems can be handled within traditional parameters.

Again, it is important to realize that if you do everything within your power to solve a problem and it just will not disappear, there needs to be a "higher rung" person(s) that will intercede. In the high school where I currently teach, we have a plethora of resource people—guidance staff, psychologists, social workers, Deans, "big brothers," etc. The list goes on and on. The more support staff that a school has, the easier your problem will be to solve. If this support does not exist, the teaching staff should try to push for it very strongly.

In addition, we have the use today of some of the "newer" techniques in school discipline, namely "peer mediation" and "conflict resolution." In these methods pupils in conflict essentially sit down face to face with one another, under the guidance of trained mediators (both teachers and peers), and try to verbally solve their problems. It is an extremely promising concept and it has its roots in some of the human relations techniques that are discussed in this book.

A well functioning, disciplined, happy class is achieved by a unique combination of many of the methods discussed in this book. It is like a stew. You taste it. It might need a bit more salt. You add it. It might need a little pepper. You add it. You try this—you try that. You ask for help from the expert chefs. You come out with a delicious dish. You're happy and so is everyone involved.

As we discussed earlier, a tear off sheet should be included with the set of rules. There should be a space for both pupil and parent to sign. An example is included in the rules at the end of this chapter. Its purpose is that of a "Learning Contract." Everyone knows what is expected of them. The pupils attach the rules to their notebooks—I have them punch holes in them for easy insertion. I also make sure that if anyone does not understand anything in the rules that they know to ask me for explanations.

Parents at times, after learning that their child owes 10 homeworks and has failed 3 tests and has cut 20 days say, "Why didn't you let me know earlier?" Very often I do. However with over 150 pupils, a middle school or secondary school teacher cannot possibly inform every parent of every problem. So, at the beginning of the term, in addition to the above set of rules, I also distribute a letter which can be found in figure 2. Basically, it informs parents that I cannot keep them updated on all data relating to their children. I let them know however, that I am always available to answer their questions and that all they have to do is call the school and leave a message, or send a note to school with their child, and I will get back to them as soon as possible. I ask parents to sign the stub attached to this letter and I keep a record of them on file. In all my years, less than one percent of parents take advantage of my offer to them to call me at school. This is unfortunate because, of course, if many parents took more of an active role in the education of their children, there would be far fewer problems in our schools today. Although I approve of teacher use of this letter, it can often cause a dilemma. The parent claims that something could've been done had they been informed, and the teacher claims that there just aren't enough hours in the day for them to call all the homes of students who are in danger of failing or in need of follow-up. Both sides have valid points. Something must be done! There are many suggestions that have been made. Keep in mind that this is a very important issue. Parents, teachers, and administrators are in a partnership. The goal is the successful functioning of the student. At PTA meetings and through flyers and newsletters home, parents should be trained in this area of their child's' education. That is, they should be aware of what is going on in school—when there are tests, holidays, report cards, etc. They should be alert to danger signals that their children might be broadcasting.

So, these make up the class rules. They must be used wisely, appropriately, and in a timely way for them to realize their full power potential as a major component in the classroom management arsenal.

FIGURE 5: "HIGH CALIBER KIDS" FLYER

"High Caliber Kids"
(A Book of Interdisciplinary Values Education)
By Mark S. Richman
(ISBN #0-9649007-1-8)

"High Caliber Kids" will help improve three problem areas that our society today must come to grips with.

The subject matter of values, getting along with others, and all aspects of trait and character development are of extreme timeliness. If this subject matter is not employed today, we may not reach tomorrow. Through this interdisciplinary book, you can teach the appreciation of basic values as well as the responsibilities we all have as members of society.

Improving communication improves cooperation. To this end, it is quite important that students enhance their skills of oral expression so that they can become more involved in helping to change our society for the better. "High Caliber Kids" aims to encourage this growth. A light sports theme is used in many of the lessons in order to keep student interest and motivation at peak levels.

"High Caliber Kids," through one of its many segments, also helps to teach the physical and psychological importance of an early program of exercise and fitness. Perhaps eventually, many of the health problems of our adult population will be eased—putting much less of a strain on our health care system.

The book is interdisciplinary. For Social Studies teachers there is the exploring of aspects of historical events and social issues. For the English staff member there are numerous articles for pupils, replete with vocabulary lists and ideas for oral discussion, speeches and role playing. Math teachers will be interested in lessons providing exploration of mathematical ideas as well as computational practice in many arithmetic concepts. Science teachers will employ lessons that detail biologic processes. Physical and Health Education teachers will enjoy lessons on exercise, physical fitness and the physiology of aerobics.

The book is very flexible. The teacher may choose to use all or only some of the lessons. Within each lesson teacher creativity should be employed to adapt and change various segments, to meet specific needs. The number of days spent on each lesson is left to the discretion of the teacher. One of the greatest assets of the book is the springboard for ideas that it provides. There are topics that may not be covered here from which lessons can be created. Every day the newspapers and magazines are full of fresh stories and issues of importance. Using my format as a guide, new lessons can be generated <u>constantly</u>. Creativity will be handsomely rewarded!

Various teaching models are suggested. These include lecture, trips, articles, videos, debates, plays, role-playing, etc.

FIGURE 6: EXCERPT FROM "HIGH CALIBER KIDS"

(For Literary Piece That Goes With This Lesson, See Figure 17)

AIM: To reflect on the events in the life of Olympic speed-skater Dan Jansen.

PERFORMANCE OBJECTIVES: The student will be able to...

1. Reflect on how performance is at times affected by psychology.

2. Realize the importance of relationships and feelings with regard to "seemingly" important things like gold medals.

3. Reflect on the tragedies of life and those in sports.

VOCABULARY:

remission, godsend, unravel, buoyed, disqualified, fiancée.

MOTIVATION:

Assign the attached piece (see page 103) to read the evening before as homework. Have pupils be ready to discuss all aspects of the story.

DEVELOPMENT:

1. Discuss the article and all of its ramifications. Encourage pupils to express their opinions, attitudes and feelings toward these and other topics:

   a. The significance of a major life event on personal performance.

   b. The importance of relationships as a priority in life.

   c. Dan's desire to donate bone marrow to his dying sister.

   d. The tragedies we all must at times deal with in life.

   e. Using family and friends as support in "difficult to cope with" situations.

HOMEWORK AND APPLICATION:

In a brief essay write your philosophy of:

    a.   The importance of relationships in your life.

    b.   Coping with tragic events.

SUMMARY:

Have students read and discuss their response to the homework assignment above.

FIGURE 7: COOL COURSE DESCRIPTION AND APPLICATION

A very important offering to the pupils is that of admission to the aforementioned "How to be Cool" Course. In order to gain entrance, an application questionnaire must be filled out: "Why do you want to be cool?" and "Which of the many cool qualities of Mr. Richman do you want to possess?" These are just two of many questions that need to be answered. Applicants must then submit to an interview. Also, two box tops from Wheaties or Cheerios must be included. In the end however, all motivated pupils are admitted to this course, which mostly takes place during pupil lunch periods or after school. In the lessons, pupils learn how to walk cool, talk cool, do math cool, look cool, dance cool, etc., with all instruction provided by the master—Mr. Richman. Some pupils can earn scholarships and thus can be admitted even without box tops. All participants learn the "cool salute" which is used to greet fellow classmates who have graduated from the class, as well as the instructor. There are usually two versions of the course—the deluxe version is for those in serious need of improvement. It is for those who are badly lacking in coolness. This particular section meets twice as many times as the standard version. The standard version of the course is for those needing only to sharpen their coolness qualities—they already are somewhat cool but want to duplicate more accurately the superior qualities of their idol—Dr. Cool Richman. A sample "Cool Course" Application is found below.

The Cool Class is a lot of fun, and is conducive to the building of great rapport between the teacher and pupils. Lessons can vary in both length and number and can be as wild or tame as creativity allows. Pupils should understand (and most do) that it is all in fun and getting "carried away" will necessarily put an end to the practice.

FIGURE 7: CONTINUED

Application for Cool Course

Answer all questions fully—use back of application or separate paper if more space is needed.

1. Name _____ Class _____

2. Why do I want to be cool?

3. Which of Mr. Richman's many cool qualities do I want most? (check all that apply)

    ☐ ability to walk cool

    ☐ his extremely cool looks

    ☐ possession of a cool brain

    ☐ having a cool hairdo

    ☐ possessing superior athletic ability

    ☐ cool dancer

    ☐ other—please specify:

4. Will you be needing a scholarship (course is $20,000 per year) or financial aid?

5. Do you want the deluxe course or the regular one? Why?

6. Do you want to learn the (check all that apply):

    a) ☐ Richman handshake

    b) ☐ Richman theme song

    c) ☐ Pledge of Allegiance to Dr. Cool Richman

7. Do you want information about the Mr. Richman fan club?

8. Which Mr. Richman merchandise do you want? (check all that apply)

    ☐ Mr. Richman Tee shirt

□ Mr. Richman coffee mug

□ Mr. Richman wrist bands

□ Mr. Richman wig

9. I need this course very badly. I must be as cool as Mr. Richman as soon as possible. Please sign me up!

10. Draw Mr. Richman on the back of this sheet.

Signature of pupil

FIGURE 8: TECHNIQUES OF INTERVIEWING

Let me take a brief detour away from holidays for a moment to discuss "interviewing." When there is a game or other "fun" time, I often do interviews with the pupils. This is a technique that requires practice. It is an art. I call a pupil up to the front and often use my ruler, yardstick or wood compass (large teacher version) as a "microphone." I ask them their name, where they live, number of brothers and sisters they have, etc. I ask their favorite subjects and favorite parts of math. They are asked if anyone is watching at home and did they bring anyone down to the studio with them? Additional math questioning then proceeds. Everyone is now smiling and enjoying and learning potential will be increased at least fifty-fold. The pupils frequently say very funny things. In addition, they learn how to express themselves and gain confidence in public speaking, factors which help to enhance their self-esteem. Students will love coming back to your class to participate more and to see their classmates participate as well. I often say that I will sign autographs at the end of the period only if a straight line is formed at the "autograph desk." Act as wildly as you are able to. The kids will love it!

FIGURE 9: EXCERPTS FROM "SURVIVE" BOOK FOR SHTICK AND MISHIGOS

Every class has rules that must be followed, work that must be covered, and tests that must be administered. However, there has to be a time for fun. I am a teacher who always injects a bit of "mishigos" (Yiddish for "craziness") into the class day. At times, this takes the form of a math game. Other times, I try to use humor at the appropriate moment. The pupils love the change of pace and they get to see that their teacher has a human side, a fun side. My relationship with them is greatly enhanced because of this approach. Other than games, riddles and jokes, I often have certain "crazy" days or unique "show biz" events. It is these "show biz" happenings or routines that I refer to as the Yiddish word "shtick." "Shtick" is Abbot and Costello doing "Who's On First" and "Niagara Falls." It is Jack Benny, when asked, "Your money or your life?" saying: "Let me think it over!" It is what "Just Let Me Survive Today" is partially about and is the purpose of this chapter.

In it will be discussed some of the wild things that are done in class. Of course not all of you will feel comfortable doing some of what I discuss here. It is meant for your consideration. Keep an open mind. Pick and choose! Do what you think might work for you. You and your pupils will love these unique events and happenings. They'll often comment: "This teacher is nuts." But you will feel the emotional bonds in your room strengthen.

First we must have a very important discussion about this chapter and correspondingly about every other chapter in this book. The ideas contained in this book have been developed gradually over my long career. They do not just "happen" in the classroom on their own. Every single "event" takes planning, creating and refining. Let me explain: Take "Elvis Day." The idea for this day, or any other "happening," comes to me from any and every source—my own ideas, a student suggestion, a TV show, etc. I then start thinking about it and how I might adapt it to my classroom teaching. Perhaps it is a TV game show that I saw. I think some more and begin writing down my ideas. I set up an almost exact minute by minute accounting of specifically how and when in the period I will proceed in class with the "event." It is similar to writing a lesson plan, or even a play. All contingencies must be considered. I start getting very excited about my game plan and its implementation.

I am at "the try it out on my best class" time of idea development. I stage it for them. Again it is fully planned out as to time and sequence and as to how I want it to develop. It works well—or perhaps miserably. I go back to the "drawing board" and refine the ideas some more. I try it out again…and again. I vary its timing, introduction, etc. It usually gets better and better each time. Finally it becomes an established piece of "shtick" or "mishigos" and it takes its place as part of my repertoire.

I have always been a "show-biz" guy and each performance for me is like another Broadway presentation before a new audience. Before "opening night" you may need to do your minute by minute rehearsal in front of a mirror or friends. Never fear failure! No matter what, you and your class will have fun. So remember this discussion as you read about the many events throughout the book! None of these activities just "happen" out of nowhere on their own. Every single one goes through a similar birth and development process. Some of this "growing-up" occurs rapidly and some quite slowly. Every "happening" is "born" in its own unique way, and is creatively raised and nurtured until it becomes ready for its "coming out." So, after lots of hard work and creativity, opening night finally takes place. With multiple refinements every one of these events eventually becomes part of the aforementioned Richman repertoire. Now, "let the games begin!"

When do these special games and activities begin? It varies according to your own creativity. At times the end of a lesson is best. At times it's right off the bat. At other times you may spontaneously begin a "shtick" activity at any moment it strikes you.

Let me begin at holidays. These are "built-in" fun days that come up at strategic times during the term. Don't ignore the explosive power that is built into holidays! We all know of the enthusiasm, good feeling and pleasure that surround holiday time at school. Anticipation builds and spirits are enhanced. This power can be harnessed to great advantage by a creative and charismatic teacher. But first, before I get into a description of holiday happenings, let me discuss a point. Of course holiday time, for some, is not the wonderful, happy time of year that I indicate here. We all know that for some pupils this time can be very lonely, sad and depressing. We must keep this in mind at these times of the year and be very sensitive to the feelings of those who might be hurting during this period. Hopefully, the spirits of most can be lifted to the greatest extent possible. We use Christmas as our first example. You should start putting up decorations a few weeks before the vacation period. Or, one could devote a part of a period to "decoration-appearing time," a time when the decorations are put up by volunteers or as a class activity. Model Santas, Christmas trees, candy canes, etc. are just some of the attractions. In any case, the pupils are gradually surrounded by increasing reminders of holiday time. As the holiday comes even closer, start injecting some music into the situation. When pupils are doing their do now exercise, for example, I play some "Jingle Bell Rock" or "All I Want for Christmas" on cassette. The students look around and start to giggle. However, inside they are having feelings which they are not accustomed to having in school. I tell them that the continuation of these songs, etc, is contingent upon their good behavior. If any pupils start getting "carried away" I remind them that they must behave for me to proceed with these unique happenings. One day I dress up as Santa and teach the class as I imagine Santa might. I then interview students asking them what they want for Christmas, mathematically. For example, do they want to improve their decimal division and multiplication, or perhaps their understanding of roman numerals?

Another game that has proven to be very popular and successful is the class horse race event. It usually takes place right before or after the topic of probability is introduced. We discuss odds and its relationship with dice, coins and now even horses. In New York there is a program at Belmont Racetrack called "Breakfast at Belmont" where school children can come to the track early in the morning and observe the horses working out. The kids are served breakfast and are addressed as to the care and grooming of the racehorse by some of the animal caregivers at the track. Gambling is not involved in this piece at all. In addition, speakers from "Gamblers Anonymous" can be brought into school to speak with the students on the horrors and pitfalls of gambling. Armed with all this knowledge, the pupils are set to get involved in the fun horse race about to unfold.

I begin by selecting about eight names for a group of horses about to "race." I pick funny names based on pupils in the class or other teachers or administrators in the school—names like "Richie-boy" (for myself, Mr. Richman) and "Sara's Dream" (for a student named Sara). I then take a piece of paper and choreograph a race. I select a winner, a leader at the half-mile pole, a leader at the top of the stretch, etc. I know who will start off slowly and who will make a great comeback. A list of the horses is prepared, odds are assigned to each and the program is distributed to the pupils. Meanwhile I tape the race on cassette behind the scenes and try to make the call of the race professional, funny and exciting. If I really want to go "all the way," I will obtain a video of a horse race and erase the sound. Then, my own voice is dubbed in referring to the horses on the tape. Either way, it is a very successful game. Pupils bet and win tickets based on the odds that have been posted. When I want to run it even more elaborately, I have some pupils acting as pari-mutuel clerks accepting bets and figuring out the payoffs. We can make it into a mini-racetrack setup. This is an example of a game that correlates well with a particular topic from the curriculum. Also, the students learn of the beauty of the racehorse as well as about some of the dangers involved in the "Sport of Kings."

FIGURE 10: LESSON PLAN FOR ELVIS DAY

Lesson Plan For Elvis Day
"Exam Preparation"

Usually, we have one aim—that for the pupils. However, here, I am also presenting a teacher ("behind the scenes") aim.

TEACHER AIM:

How can we use "Elvis Day" as a way of motivating exam preparation for pupils?

PUPIL AIM:

What can we learn from the life and times of Elvis?

PERFORMANCE OBJECTIVE:

The student will be able to…

1. Make use of the Elvis character to create a positive and fun atmosphere for learning.

MOTIVATION:

1. We preface the motivation by mentioning some aspects of "journal writing". Expressing one's thoughts in a written manner is an important component of mathematics education. To this end, pupils should be trained in this area early in the term, by maintaining a journal. In this journal, pupils can write of their thoughts and feelings on various aspects of the mathematics as well as of their thought processes in solving various math problems.

2. To motivate Elvis Day we have a several-pronged approach. On the do now assignment, in their journals, have pupils answer the following questions: a) Why is it important to do well on the upcoming exam? b) What factors might cause me not to study well and/or to do poorly on the exam?, c) How can I prevent these situations from occurring?

3. In addition, several weeks before this lesson, assign students to read various books or magazine articles on different aspects of the life and times of Elvis Presley.

4. To set the tone for Elvis Day and to get the festivities underway, while the do now is in progress, i.e., at the beginning of the period, be dressed in your complete Elvis attire and set the tone by playing one of Elvis' great hits—preferably "Are You Lonesome Tonight?" Concurrently, parade around the classroom holding up, mounted on cardboard, pictures of the 2 released Elvis stamps (or his photos)—the young and old versions of the King. Ham up the event as much as you can! Have pupils join you in the singing at critical points! The children really do enjoy these unique happenings. Try to conduct the entire lesson—from do now through the end—in Elvis voice and manner. (Ladies, unless you can do an Elvis imitation yourself, you may have to invite an Elvis-impersonator guest to help you out today).

DEVELOPMENT:

1. Elicit the aim from students at this time. You might have some speeches made either by you or by guests highlighting the life and times of the King. You might also show some Elvis film clips or videotapes, or play some of his greatest hits.

2. At first focus on some of the positive aspects of Elvis' career—how he rose to the top through hard work and talent. Talk about his great singing voice and magnificent charisma. Do this via any number of ways—lecture, guests, speeches, highlight pieces, etc.

3. Elvis (you or a suitable replacement) then leads the class in a discussion of some specific methods of exam preparation and study techniques. Touch on time budgeting, study methods, tips, mnemonics, and any other methods that you think might be of help to your pupils.

4. Then begin discussing some of the problems that arose in Elvis' life. Mention what they were, what may have caused them, and what effects they had on Elvis' career and life. Also, you can speculate with the class on how some of these problems might have been prevented or alleviated.

5. Lead the class into a parallel discussion on problems that might arise in a student's life that perhaps would interfere with studying or even lead to failure on exams. Discuss how these problem areas might be prevented or worked on. During this more serious part of the discussion, the option exists for the teacher to also become more serious, and even to temporarily suspend Elvis

festivities (i.e., voice and other comedic aspects of the day). Or, one can maintain the mood yet try still to reinforce the theme of the lesson.

6. At the conclusion of this developmental lesson, give out song sheets and have all join in for the singing of some of Elvis' greatest hits—led by the chief Elvis impersonators—be it you or whomever.

SUMMARY:

1. What did you get from Elvis Day?

2. Summarize your methods of exam preparation by listing the exact steps you would take to get set for the upcoming examination.

3. What problems and road blocks might prevent you from succeeding in school?

4. Take out your journal and jot down your thoughts about this entire lesson.

HOMEWORK AND APPLICATION:

1. Write up a daily time budget that you can use to prepare for the upcoming exam.

2. Explain why it is so important to have this guideline and to stick to it.

3. List what you plan to study during each time block.

4. List the names of some famous people (from show business, sports, etc.) whose fame and success have faded because of their use of drugs or other problems. Write a brief summary about the problem.

5. Read a book on the life of someone you mentioned in question 4 and write a brief report on this person.

6. Plan for "Imitation Day" where pupils choose a famous character (even Mr. Richman) and the student leads the class in some "lesson on living" that the character chosen might be able to teach the class. Prizes might be awarded to the best, most creative, etc.

7. Register for a course in "How to Study" or "Improving your Memory" which might help in sharpening study skills.

FIGURE 11: EXCERPT FROM HIGH CALIBER KIDS ON THE OLYMPICS

(See Figure 17 For The Piece That Goes With This Lesson)

AIM: To (possibly) view on videotape and to read about the Olympic Men's Figure Skating Competition that became known as the "Battle of the Brians" of 1988.

PERFORMANCE OBJECTIVES: The student will be able to...

1. Explore one's emotions in handling pressure, defeat, disappointment, victory and success.

2. Answer the "Great Question: "What is success?"

3. Appreciate the beauty of figure skating.

4. Investigate some of the many components of competition—hard work, sacrifice, camaraderie, faith, and the channeling of one's emotions.

VOCABULARY:

Achilles heel, gratifying, poignant, flawlessly, camaraderie.

MOTIVATION:

The evening before the lesson, have the students read the attached piece (see figure 17) on the figure skating finals. On the first day of the lesson, show the Olympic videotape of the '88 men's competition—try contacting ABC Sports for a copy. You might even want to contact the International Olympic Committee. If you cannot obtain this specific tape, get one on virtually any Olympic Games—these should be available at video stores.

DEVELOPMENT:

Discuss the following points that follow in sequence in the reading (and tape-viewing):

1. Contrast the different ways that Orser and Boitano had to handle the enormous pressure on them. Include mention of sports psychologists and support networks. Is it better to perform first or second in competi-

tion? How do you deal with pressure situations in your own life? Discuss various aspects of this critical question.

2. How did Boitano feel after skating flawlessly in the long program? Why did he look up skyward?

3. How do you feel, after working very hard on a task, when it is successfully completed? After Boitano's great performance, why did winning the gold not seem that important?

4. Discuss Orser's final performance in relation to how you feel before a big test.

5. How did Orser handle defeat? How do you handle losing?

6. At the awards ceremony, what do you think was the relationship between the Brians? How do you relate to your competitors?

7. Discuss the vocabulary words.

8. What does it mean to "channel your emotions?" Do you think Boitano was successful at this task?

9. What did success really mean to Brian Boitano? What, to you, is success? Is it happiness, material wealth, etc.?

10. Why do you think Orser lost the gold medal?

11. Where do sacrifice and faith enter into this story?

HOMEWORK AND APPLICATION:

You are going to interview the Brians for a sports TV interview show. Compose a series of questions including the following information:

1. handling pressure.

2. working long and hard toward a goal.

3. handling disappointment and/or defeat.

4. any other questions you believe to be appropriate.

You might even consider performing mock interviews with classmates using similar questions. Other questions might center on:

5. the necessity of sacrifice to achieve what you seek, and—

6. the part that faith might play in the entire matter.

SUMMARY:

Discuss what you learned from the "Battle of the Brians."

FIGURE 12: MORE LESSONS FROM "HIGH CALIBER KIDS"

AIM: Should Athletes Be Allowed to Leave College Early To Turn Pro?

PERFORMANCE OBJECTIVES: The student will be able to...

1. Investigate a real life decision—making situation via cooperative learning and role-playing.

2. Come to more clearly understand the dynamics involved in decision making.

MOTIVATION:

You are offered ten million dollars to leave college after one year and become a New York Knick. Write in your journal your decision and reasons for it.

DEVELOPMENT:

In a cooperative learning experience, divide the class up into groups. Each group will represent one aspect of the situation discussed in the Aim. The group will get together, crystallize its philosophy on the issue, and choose a representative to express its philosophy. In the subsequent role-play situation, a large round table will be used and each representative will have a chance to deliver his (or her) position (with reference to the Aim). The other groups will be given a chance to "grill" the speaker. The various groups will each represent one of the following protagonists in this issue:

1. the athlete in question

2. the athlete's parent(s)

3. the athlete's agent

4. the current college coach

5. the former high school coach

6. the university president

7. teachers in the high school and college attended by the pupil

8. the pro team owner

9. a member of the press

10. the President of the NCAA Committee

11. the girlfriend

12. the best friend

13. the fan

Try to see to it that the role-play situation touches on most of the following issues:

1. Obligations (moral and otherwise) that the pupil might have (or feel) to his college, his parents, himself.

2. The education that the pupil may or may never receive.

3. Role model behavior expected by relatives, friends and youngsters in the community.

Arrange the Q&A session as a "TV talk-show" format. Have a host!

HOMEWORK AND APPLICATION:

1. Set up a debate situation for this topic. Have pupils assume the positions of both sides and have an actual debate.

2. Write a play involving all components of this interesting situation.

3. Have pupils investigate the final educations obtained by student-athletes who have graduated early—did they go back to finish college?

4. Write a New York Times—type editorial of the policy that you think should be finalized in this situation.

SUMMARY:

What did you learn about policy-making from today's lesson?

FIGURE 13: LESSON ON A DAY AT THE RACES

AIM: To enjoy breakfast at Belmont Racetrack (or any racetrack) and learn about the beauty of the thoroughbred racehorse.

PERFORMANCE OBJECTIVES: The student will be able to…

1. Appreciate the beauty of the thoroughbred racehorse.

2. Enjoy all aspects of a beautiful pastoral setting in springtime and learn about the sport of horseracing from a non-gambling aspect.

3. Learn about the care and respect of animals.

VOCABULARY:

During the trip many new words will be used. The teacher will keep a list of new words and in a subsequent lesson review their meaning and significance.

MOTIVATION:

On the evening before the actual trip, assign for homework the following topic for a brief essay: "What are your thoughts and feelings when you hear the word "racetrack?" The purpose of this is to compare the thoughts of pupils both before and after the trip. The contrast might be dramatic. You might want to brief students on what they will be seeing during the trip—or possibly save it as an exciting surprise.

DEVELOPMENT:

1. This lesson is basically a trip to Belmont Park. The season opens in early May and runs through the end of the school semester. Students are given a multi-faceted program. They are educated in the daily routine of the horses, the training of the animals for aspects of their sport, and are given a tour of the barn facilities with lectures on the treatment of the equine athletes. There are question and answer sessions offered by trained guides. The students have a delicious breakfast overlooking the track with the opportunity to observe the horses going through their early-morning workouts. There are giveaways and a well-structured program is provided. If one wants details of the program, contact Belmont Park in Elmont L.I., N.Y. If your town does not have a similar program, perhaps you can help to arrange one. In any event, hopefully this lesson

might inspire you to create similar opportunities for corresponding lessons on this or other sports trips.

2. In the performance objectives we have indicated various goals of this event. There are more that should be worked into discussion on a subsequent day. Students should focus on some of the following:

    a. Enjoy and observe the atmosphere and excitement of the early-morning track routines.

    b. Enjoy breakfast while watching a superb athletic performance.

    c. Learn about the daily routine of the thoroughbred racehorse.

    d. Begin to think in terms of job opportunities in the animal kingdom.

    e. Observe how even horses must receive education and training in their jobs.

    f. Think about gambling and how it would detract from the beauty that you are now observing.

    g. Appreciate the sport for its beauty in addition to as a business.

APPLICATION AND HOMEWORK:

1. For homework prepare a written or oral report dealing with how your ideas have changed (since the trip) on hearing the word "racetrack."

2. Be prepared to discuss what you have learned today (refer to development and objectives) as well as vocabulary and racetrack jargon.

3. Would you recommend a trip to the track for a friend or family member?

4. A future trip to the track during actual race conditions to observe the athletes at work might be scheduled.

5. Arrange for a later lesson calling on the services of a representative from Gambler's Anonymous to illustrate the negative aspects of horseracing.

SUMMARY:

1. What would you tell future classes who go to "Breakfast at Belmont" to look for on their trip? Include much of what you learned as reflected in the development.

FIGURE 14: TECHNIQUES OF TALKING TO PARENTS—EXCERPT FROM "SURVIVE BOOK"

Throughout the book I have touched on "parental involvement." Of course, having help from parents is extremely important. We have spoken about getting to know your students. Also, get to know their parents! How? Often guidance, administration and/or other teachers can shed light upon pupil home situations. It helps, before making home contact, to know something about whom you will be dealing with. Once you decide on contacting the parent there are a few important points to consider. We discussed parental phone calls previously in the "Rules" Chapter, but it is so important, that I will briefly touch on it again here.

The best method of home contact is via the telephone. You are "live" and there is much less chance for misunderstanding of information. You can have a dialogue, a give and take, and this is always important. Do not call when you are angry—sit down and make an outline of what you plan to say. Call when you can easily talk—not when you are in a rush or from a place that is very noisy. Always begin by saying something positive. Then discuss the problem. End the conversations on an encouraging note. Let the parent know that there is hope, that there is potential for improvement and that you want to work together as a team to effect change.

Very rarely, if you go about your conversation in the non-confrontational positive way outlined above, will you have an unpleasant phone call. Often, an effective outcome will result.

Many parents do not know what is going on in school—or do not want to face it or perhaps do not know what to do about it. You may need to refer them to the guidance department and/or administration for further follow-up. They may need referrals to counseling or outside agencies that can help their children. Usually these referrals can be made by appropriate school personnel. Always bring to the attention of your school support teams any information which you derive from a telephone call that you think they should know regarding abuse, drugs or really anything else that might be pertinent. Lives can be saved! Always keep a record of telephone calls.

As mentioned, letter writing, although it has its place in some cases, does not come close to having the effect and value of the phone call. In the rare case of a negative parental response, simply discuss the problem with your supervisor and let him follow up.

In order to increase your involvement with parents, join the PTA and attend as many meetings as possible. See to it that pupils take home all important notices that are generated by the school and that they do not wind up in the class garbage can. Try to educate parents on how to become involved in and monitor their children's' education.

FIGURE 15: PRIZE PHILOSOPHY

The prizes or awards are a very important component of this program. Your own philosophies and creativity will help this segment take shape.

As pupils win contests, games, and competitions, they are awarded tickets (also known as points). For example, they might accumulate 25 points in a week. Each game is worth a different number of points.

A pupil might win five points for "The Price Is Right" game and another ten for "Family Feud". A math contest might then enrich him by 20 points, especially if three students prior to his giving the winning answer were unable to correctly answer the question (the jackpot thus builds). The student would have then accumulated 35 points.

A roster of names is kept and on it are recorded the total point values for each pupil. Lists are posted in the room or distributed so that pupils know how many points they have. Points can be, if desired, converted into paper "tickets" and given to the students, similar to money. With their accumulated points or tickets they can "buy" prizes and rewards.

What do tickets look like? Again the art work is up to you but in figure 30 (Survive Book), a sample is offered of what a Mr. Richman ticket looks like. On it there are spaces for the value that it is worth, what it has been awarded for and the name of the pupil. In the past, some sly pupils have attempted to counterfeit tickets. Only by superior law enforcement techniques and excellent detective work, was I able to bust these illegal activities and deal out punishment and rehabilitation.

Just what kind of prizes are we talking about? There are many different types. First, I like to find out what it is that my pupils want. Of course, within reason. Very popular in the past have been: sweat wrist bands, sweat head bands, batting gloves, posters, tapes, athletic equipment, stuffed animals, and baseball cards, among many other items. Grand prizes have been basketballs and walkmen. I usually compile a list of prizes with required number of points or tickets that pupils must accumulate to win each.

When can the prizes be won? It is up to you. Some years I allow students to turn in their tickets (converted from points) at any time during the term. Other times I only permit it at holiday time. And yet other years, pupils must wait until the end of the term to claim their winnings.

How much should you spend on buying prizes? Again, it is totally up to you. In addition to using your own money I can suggest other ways to raise funds: 1) Grant-writing, 2) Getting parent groups involved in raising money, and/or 3)

Using various fund raising techniques such as selling candy, etc. When you use you own funds, it can be costly, but to me, it is certainly worth the investment. The dividends can be enormous. Consult your tax accountant since these items may at times be deducted as business expenses. Again, the amount of money you spend is totally within your control. You can have pupils save as few or as many tickets as you desire to purchase various prizes. In fact, with some classes, expensive gifts are not needed at all. For example, some pupils love certificates, buttons, pencils, pens, trophies, award ceremonies, seeing their names up on the wall, having lunch with the teacher, having a pizza party, having no homework for a day, getting a free period or any number of other inexpensive rewards.

This entire segment of my program again calls for your own individual teacher creativity.

I advise pupils who want to save their tickets over the summer that when they do so their tickets accumulate interest at 10-20%. Students learn strategies of saving and a little about investing. They can then turn them in the following year to purchase something even more valuable. Believe it or not, I have had pupils returning to visit me after 10-15 years saying that they have saved their tickets and wanting to know how much are they worth today? Lots! Recently, I have even had as a pupil in my class the daughter of a former student. Soon tickets will be passed on down through the generations!

My monitors are often "paid" with tickets. Lost tickets often are not replaced. I urge pupils to keep them, like money, in a safe place. A few years ago, one sad pupil came to me with tickets that had completely faded print on them—his mother had washed his jeans and yes, the tickets inside as well. Exceptions are made and his "cleaned" tickets were replaced.

FIGURE 16: MY CAREER IN EDUCATION

Armed with fifteen years of camping experience and <u>no</u> student teaching, I became a New York City math teacher.

That first year was "trial by fire." Everything was extremely difficult. The pupils were so hard to control. I was required to take a "beginning teacher's course" and there I would go each week and commiserate with all the other new teachers. However, I learned a lot from this course. I received pointers and suggestions from my enthusiastic and sympathetic colleagues and from the veteran mentors who knew how things should be done.

Then I met up with a seasoned Dean of Discipline at my school who was known for her strictness and "meanness." One day after school she sat down with me and for hours discussed her ideas on discipline as well as her classroom management techniques. She had an enormous number of excellent suggestions. There were some parts of her presentation that were not suitable for my personality. This is an important point in the art of teaching. Ask for help. Ask for tips. But do not think that you have to copy advice "word for word." Listen. Take what is appropriate for you. Find your comfort zone!

The next fourteen years I'll call the "trial and error—get better" years. I taught five classes of junior high school pupils every day. And I learned! I attended workshops, seminars, took courses and networked. I had "good" classes, "bad" classes, nice kids, troubled kids, rough days, easy days, snow days, rain days, large groups and small groups. I developed games, puzzles, survival strategies and management techniques. I rubbed elbows with great teachers, good teachers, poor teachers, great leaders and poor leaders. I tried new ideas and new methods. Some worked and some did not. The "trial and error—get better" years—a fourteen year professional growing experience!

Then, almost suddenly, things started to happen. I decided to go back to school and received a masters degree in educational administration. That was a stimulating and wonderful experience. I applied for and received an "Impact II Developer Grant" from the New York City Board of Education, on which this book is based. That opened up new paths for me.

I then applied for the position of "Dean of Discipline" at my junior high school. Although I had an excellent reputation as a teacher, the administration reluctantly gave me the job. They believed that "students should tremble with fear" when they were sent to the Dean. My philosophy was discipline with dignity and basically counter to theirs. Two years later the administration named me "Teacher of the Year."

My experience as Dean certainly was the most powerful and influential on me as an educator to that point in my career. I believe it also uniquely qualifies me to write this book. As Dean, I did just about everything an educator could ever want to do—could ever want to see. I often think of the Christmas movie—"It's A Wonderful Life:" Where would many students be now if I had not touched their lives? And we teachers all could and should feel that way. It is a unique gift available to members of our profession.

First I was put in charge of the pupil cafeteria. This gave me great experience in large group control. General Norman Schwartzkopff himself might have trouble leading a student lunchroom. We had to feed 300 students in forty-five minutes and assure that all the students were safe and happy. I handled most disciplinary matters for grades six through nine. I had an opportunity to conduct hundreds of one-on-one interviews with children. I learned to listen to their side of the story.

I had to mediate disputes between parents, pupils, teachers and administrators. I saw evidence of child abuse, drug use, teen pregnancy and suicide. I was a doctor, a referee, a nurse, a psychiatrist, a social worker and a friend. I gave advice. I asked for advice. I learned. I provided crisis intervention for students and staff. I compiled reports, anecdotes and dossiers. I was a detective, a cop and a judge. I was involved with the New York City Police and Transit Police, the Department of Social Services, the courts, the New York City hospitals, and the local neighborhood associations. I learned more about special education and bilingual education. I learned about gangs and violence. I drove fearful students home. I saw students and teachers cry and I cried with them. I learned how to secure a school.

I was active in parent's association affairs and learned what concerns parents had in our school. I helped organize events and trips. In other words—it broadened my educational experience tremendously. And this is one very important ingredient in pedagogical improvement: Experience!

I then began presenting my ideas and techniques at many staff development conferences in New York City. This culminated in 1993 in my being invited to three states by the National Council of Math Teachers to present my program at their regional conferences, the highlight of which was an unforgettable three hour mini-course in Columbus, Georgia.

Over the past 5 years, I have become a high school math teacher. It has provided me with the great opportunity to follow the development and maturation of the junior high school/middle-school student.

In addition, several years ago, I was a finalist in the "Funniest Teacher in New York City" contest held by a local comedy club.

Now that you know more about me, I hope that it will help you to understand much of the program that will be presented in the pages that follow.

That was basically my story as of the initial printing of this book. However, here in 2006, so much has happened vis a vis my experiences in education that it has become essential that I add much more to this chapter (and book). In addition, the reason I cover all this education detail in a camp counselor manual is that the two fields are so much related. Each field helps one to understand the other.

In 1997, I became Assistant Principal at Erasmus High School which will be the topic of another book. Then, from 1997 through 2000, I performed staff and curriculum development for the schools of Brooklyn and Staten Island and in February 2001, I returned to the classroom to teach math full-time (and become an "in-house" staff development person).

This latter experience provided me with the enormously amazing opportunity to be a "rookie" teacher in a school (but a "special" rookie—one possessing 27 years of experience) who had the opportunity to perform "battle duty."

As just mentioned, when this book had its first printing (in '95), I had been at Lincoln HS for three years. Let me pick up now at the remainder of my career at Lincoln and move onto the next phase of my experiences (as introduced above).

At Lincoln High School, I spent five glorious years in my first (non summer) High School experience. I served as my unions' chapter leader which involved me in lots of day to day conflicts between teachers and administrators. This gave me the experience that helped teach me how to settle disagreements between people with (at times greatly) differing viewpoints on usually quite controversial and/or emotionally—charged issues.

This "expertise" helped sharpen my skills in settling disputes between pupils who often were involved in remarkably similar interpersonal disputes, in working with gang members and in other potentially volatile situations. At the time I began teaching at Lincoln, my great chairman, Harold Kornblum, encouraged me to get involved in teaching a most rigorous course—Advanced Placement Calculus. Since I hadn't taken this class since college, it motivated me to learn massive amounts of very complicated material and quickly teach it to a group of 25 very gifted children, who would challenge me with major league questions.

This occurrence was yet another wonderful "growing" experience in my career. It helped me learn how to investigate, prepare and refine unfamiliar curricula—and adapt it to the demands of a most challenging and gifted group of youngsters. It helped put me "in the shoes" of my target population and helped me handle quite a stressful situation.

The graphing calculator was another major new ingredient—I had never used it before, and mastery of its use was required on the AP Calculus Exam. Many of my pupils, growing up in the computer age, were extremely adept with this technology and I even took "lessons" (during my lunch period) from some of them. It was a year of extremely hard work—preparing very intricate material for "double" periods totaling 90 minutes per day.

Some of the brighter pupils constantly challenged me, often "showing off" by trying to "show me up." Often I needed to prepare into the "wee hours" of the night for these gambits by day. There were major rewards however, when large percentages of my class fared exceedingly well on the most challenging AP exam. It also reinforced my belief in always taking on new challenges—no matter how intimidating or threatening. These experiences are golden in trying to mold one's character and in making one a much better educator. I also encourage all of my pupils and colleagues to constantly take on new challenges and to always "go for it."

At Lincoln HS I had a wonderful position. I was teaching some wonderful children in calculus class and in algebra and served as the union representative for my school. Still, I left. Over the summer of 1997, I had received a call from the Principal of a really tough inner city High School in Brooklyn NY called Erasmus Hall High School. This school had lots of problems—dropouts, poor academic results, gangs, fighting—you name it. I was asked to become the Assistant Principal in charge of Guidance, Security and Math. I decided to take this (potentially) very stressful job. It was in keeping with my philosophy of "go for it." It would give me 30 years of experience in one year–and it did!!

As Assistant Principal of Guidance, on a daily basis I dealt with an almost constant stream of serious disciplinary situations–gang involvement, fights, and security issues of quite an intense level. I learned so much that year—about graduation requirements, transcripts, family problems, etc. I dealt with police, hospitals, family courts, probation officers. I learned to deal with very hardcore tough disciplinary cases. It helped me to become a better classroom and school wide disciplinarian. I ran a lunchroom in which 800 pupils dined at one time in one (quite large) room. This experience taught me that I could handle almost anything.

There were challenging decisions daily that had to be made one after another. In fact, there were so many that they became "easy" to deal with. It sharpened my decision—making abilities—under stress.

The pupils and teachers loved me, trusted me, and respected me. I gave all the same respect and kindness. But you know what? It became a bit depressing after a while dealing day after day with discipline problems and crime related issues. I longed to return to more academically oriented pursuits. That's when the next call came. After working nineteen years at the same school, I was about to accept my fourth new job in seven years. Change was good for me—it kept my world exciting and my mind and soul growing quite positively. I suggest it for everyone from time to time.

That call came in late spring 1998. Would you like to assume the exciting role of math staff and curriculum development specialist for most of the High Schools in Brooklyn and Staten Island NY? You would be training teachers in methods of teaching math to all levels of students, you'd be developing curriculum, giving hundreds of workshops, attending just as many, learning about cutting edge studies on brain research, cooperative learning strategies, among many other stimulating items; you'd be traveling city-wide, state-wide, country-wide, meeting hundreds of different people and lots of teachers and administrators; you'd be able to write, create—learn all about the latest methods of monitoring students and study techniques. Every day you will wake up and you'll be like a kid in a candy store of educational opportunity. You bet I'll accept!

This position led to nearly three years of further personal and professional growth. But once again I was removed from actual classroom involvement. One can begin to drift and become "out of touch." In New York City at the time (about 2000-2001) there were large groups of students who were failing the HS "exit" exam (the "Regents" exam), an exam required for graduation. The curriculum folks developed a unique idea. They would send those (mostly) seniors to summer school from July 1st through August 17th—and tailor 3 hour intensive math class instruction for them every day.

The thinking was that these "supersized" (time wise) classes might provide the necessary blitz of knowledge. Most teachers felt it a crazy idea to take these kids who had failed algebra numerous times (and in many cases were severe behavior problems) and subject them (and their teacher) to three hours of continuous instruction. I thought so too but nothing else had worked. A problem though: No one really wanted to teach the class or, for that matter, was trained or equipped to do so. I was asked to write a training manual for this class, for there would be perhaps forty or so of these classes city-wide.

In preparing the manual I literally had to "walk through" the three hour lesson 30 times in order to cover the entire year's material. I realized that teaching this class would be enormously challenging and truly doubted its success. But, I also became quite excited thinking that I might perhaps pilot teach this class. Yes! How could I write an accurate roadmap for other teachers if I did not instruct this class and play with my ideas in actual practice? So I did. During the summers of 2000 and 2001, I taught this 7 week summer course to seniors who needed to pass this algebra exam to graduate. And how stimulating and rewarding it was!! I was back in the classroom under pressure to succeed and to succeed with pupils who had failed miserably to this point.

Mostly, I called upon my 30 years of educational experience—the ideas contained in this book. I followed chapter and verse: "Just Let Me Survive Today!" I used my techniques of human relations. I also had pupils play math games, win prizes, do targeted practice exercises and drill. I had a student teacher for the first time in 30 years—an enthusiastic college student about to become a teacher himself who helped enormously and who related to my pupils very effectively. Always volunteer to get a student teacher if the possibility arises.

However, recall now that I had not been in the classroom for the past four years. I'd been an administrator and staff and curriculum developer. But I had learned so much in those last four years and now was the time to bring all this learning to the classroom.

I'd learned about the latest ideas from the world of "brain research." I knew now that pupil understanding could be even more enhanced by cooperative learning—by working together in small groups and helping one another. The kids needed study skills strategies. I created many mnemonics—and other little tricks to help them memorize necessary formulas and facts. Most pupils loved to dance and listen to music so we put many of the mathematical formulas "to music" and created dance steps to make the learning more fun and much more effective.

The 3 hour classes went by so quickly. Each daily session was broken up into various parts—first a lecture, then a math game. We followed this by a cooperative learning session, an open-book quiz, some dancing and singing, another game, another mini-lecture, and wrapped it up by using a "math cheer," a quiz or a massive bingo math review game. Every day was a Broadway Extravaganza. In addition, we used the USA Today to link the math to "real-world" events and practices.

In addition, we injected much from the world of technology—using the internet to help us develop lesson strategies and targeted math recreation. Technology in the form of calculators (scientific and graphing) was introduced and taught at critical junctures to help enhance pupil understanding. I received a grant on the use of technology in the classroom.

Along the lines of study strategies, pupils were taught how to take notes while reading and while in class and how to organize these notes so that they could become effective tools for learning. Many other study skills strategies were implemented, which is the subject of an upcoming book.

All pupils (including special education along with those with "learning disabilities") enhanced their methods of study by leaps and bounds. Most pupils previously had no conception of any of this studying methodology. Most pupils, I find, really want to do well. However, they often lack the study skills that will ensure the best chance for success.

Finally, August 17th and the exit exam (the NY State "Regents") day had arrived. Amazingly, over 70% of the class (of about 36 pupils) passed the exam. Many others came very close. A "miracle" had occurred in Brooklyn. I was onto something-big.

I spent 6 more months as a staff developer, bringing enhanced enthusiasm and realism to my presentation. I had actually been successful. Yes, "all students can learn," a phrase I had repeated (yet never truly believed) for years. I truly now believed it and this was an amazing revelation for me. My workshops became much more exciting as I enthusiastically delivered presentations that were now truly ingrained in my heart and soul.   *THEORY + PRACTICE!*

By the spring of 2001 I had succumbed to the teaching "bug" completely. I needed to be in the classroom full time to experiment and practice with my strategies. The classroom would become my laboratory where I would experiment and practice my craft—my art. In addition, it seemed that teachers often had little time in their busy and stressful days to sit and hear lectures from a non-practicing staff developer (like myself) who had a "cushy" "distinct office" job (as they often viewed it), never getting his hands dirty in the everyday teaching grind. I needed to be among them once again. Additionally, I would have more time to converse with colleagues and they would pay much more attention to one (i.e., me) going through the same day-to-day stresses!

So, in February, 2001, I returned to the classroom full time—not only in summertime. The site was Automotive HS, a (nearly) all boys vocational school in Brooklyn, NY—a school on the verge of "shut down" due to poor academic results—a school in "redesign" with one last chance to reverse its fortunes.

There was a new principal and a veteran (very competent—dedicated) Assistant Principal of Mathematics and Science (who would later become a Principal herself). Yes, I was back in the classroom once again in quite a difficult inner city school. But you know what? I loved it! I brought those same wonderful summer school strategies to "Auto." The kids loved the methods and a school that most teachers avoided at any cost, to me, was heaven.

What I saw was a needy student population with a group of truly dedicated and caring teachers trying to reverse a history of failure and coming up against all sorts of difficult odds—lack of money, budget cuts, and really tough students mostly used to failure. Yet the teachers, through meeting after meeting, idea after idea and dedication and spirit like I had not seen (too often) before, gradually were piecing the school back together into a hopeful place with lots of potential.

For me, the term gave another challenging opportunity to work my strategies with yet more students who most had been "written off" by most. Even more challenging was that this time many were not seniors so their backs were not "up against the wall." Motivation and spirit were needed much more in this school. In addition, as mentioned, I had the amazingly unique opportunity to be treated like a rookie teacher in a school—yet one with 30 years or so of vast educational experience. It gave me the chance (using my experience and insight) to lay back and gradually observe the inner workings (both positive and negative) of a school and to try and contribute ideas that might help the school turn the corner and succeed more effectively. This term's experience certainly showed me that a united faculty dedicated to improving their lot and that of their pupils certainly can help to improve conditions for all and make it a more hopeful and positive place in which to work.

One major example was a union created "Teacher Center" at Automotive. It was a huge room made for teachers only. Here teachers could go, before, after, and during school, and do any lesson planning, test grading, eating, relaxing and using the excellent and available duplicating facilities. They could relax and "schmooze," use the phone, and enjoy coffee and snacks any time of day. They could observe workshops or watch TV. The great asset however, was that this large and well-staffed and maintained (by a union member whose sole job was to manage this room and provide major emotional and academic support for teachers) room provided a major oasis for staff during their busy and stressful day. No school I'd been in before or since had this truly amazing set up! It helped make a hugely stressful situation much more palatable. It was heaven is what it was.

My Automotive period was quite challenging and enlightening. The point of the "Teacher Center anecdote" is that teachers need to push to establish this kind of atmosphere—where they can relax, unwind and prepare for their classes in other than the often traditional cramped and demoralizing situation.

Self-love → Similar to Allies taking care of themselves

The summer of 2001 took me back for another successful summer school tour, again with those three hour classes. And, the numbers were quite positive, reflecting further academic success. My system had now proven the test of time.

Automotive High School made it six different highly unique positions over a nine year time period. As mentioned, varying positions and jobs like this helped me stay focused and full of excitement and spirit.

Then in late August 2001, I received yet another call. Would I like to become Assistant Principal (again) of Math, Science and Economics and Finance—at the High School of Economics and Finance in downtown Manhattan—only one block from the World Trade Center? Well, it would again take me "out of the classroom" (except for teaching one calculus class) and into the arms of administration. It was a school with ten floors located in an office building in the heart of the financial district of New York City. It had major involvement with some of the largest financial institutions in the world. It was New York City—The Big Apple!! After 29 years I had finally made it to (near) Broadway—full time. Of course I would accept—it was a wonderful opportunity to become part of a cutting edge and potentially enormous growth situation.

After only a few days on this most challenging and stimulating job, I was having a conversation with my principal when we heard a "BOOM" outside. The building shook. I immediately thought—"bomb." As it turned out, it was about 9 AM, and it was 9/11/01, and we were at 100 Trinity Place—right across the street from the "Twin Towers." You know much of the rest—or do you?? We had over 700 pupils in our building. We were not permitted to evacuate as there was falling debris and potential disaster on the street. We felt new respect for our well—run fire/shelter drills as most kept calm amid a background of horrible reports that we were beginning to hear.

This is yet another aspect of education. Amid crises and even disaster we must model calm leadership to help our children cope. After the second plane hit the tower, we were given orders to evacuate. We marched our 700 pupils and staff down up to ten stairwells and out of the building. There was falling debris (and even bodies) as we wound our way through the streets of (a fairly unfamiliar area for me) lower NYC.

We all gathered near the "Bowling Green" subway station when suddenly the first tower began to (unbelievably) collapse. It sent a hurricane of swirling debris right in our direction (or, basically every direction). We all took off. It was terrifying as we became separated and eventually were covered with little particles of eye and face burning "dust." Which way to run? Is everyone OK? Will we live? Will we go blind as our eyes closed to small slits as the unthinkable unfolded?

Well, the remaining hours and even days can serve as the material for another book down the road.

It turns out, we all miraculously survived–much of it due to the leadership and bravery under pressure exhibited by our staff and students. We could not return to our damaged school building for over seven months. During this period I again received an education in leadership and survival.

We had to share a building with Norman Thomas High School, located in midtown Manhattan. The big problem was that we had to wait to begin our school day until their shortened day had ended. This resulted for us in a quite difficult curtailed school day (for nearly seven months) that began about 1:30 PM and ended at approximately 6 PM.

When we finally resumed classes a couple of weeks after 9/11 at our new site, we began with almost no textbooks (everything was back at our original site), hardly any duplicating facilities—and the school year was still only in its extreme early stages. It turned out to be an unbelievably challenging year, to put it quite mildly. We received millions of dollars in grants and were the subject of TV and radio shows, newspaper articles and honors. The psychological effects were certainly, in some cases, major. But we did all pull together like a family that had survived a horrible situation—and we emerged as a strong team. We did give 110% and had an amazing year, doing the best that could be expected of anyone in that situation.

I received a "crash course" in administration. I learned, under extreme pressure, how to deal with emergencies, choose and order textbooks (thousands of them), and help to program a school. From what appeared to be an overwhelmingly impossible situation we turned things around, stabilized them and moved forward, trying to salvage (and we did succeed at that) an entire school year. Of course, in cases as this (in education and in life), we emerged truly stronger for having been through this horror. And so it is as a teacher—rookie or veteran—there will be (sometimes) minor and at times major ups and downs. One must remain positive, focused, dedicated, professional, resilient and, above all, one must persevere!! You will emerge a stronger teacher, a better teacher, a better person. And your pupils will emerge better prepared to face the challenges that life has to offer.

Another stressful year as an administrator rather successfully patching together a broken situation. I needed to get out of NY City (Manhattan) at this point. I had moved to Millburn New Jersey (big commute from here to NYC) and seized on the opportunity to once again return to teaching full time. I secured a position as a math teacher in a school much closer to my new home—Port Richmond HS in Staten Island, NY.

It was now fall or 2002. Every single one of my 130 pupils had failed math the previous year and were "repeaters." They came with the usual cartload of personal, academic and emotional problems. It was time for me once again to rise to the challenge. I was, as mentioned, now in Staten Island NY, one of the outer boroughs of New York City. So, I spent these final two years of my NYC career at Port Richmond HS in Staten Island—a school with a long history—built many decades ago. The pupils were every bit as challenging as those I struggled with back in September of 1973. Although "the times they have been a—changing," the basic nature of the child has not. Kids still responded very well to fun, games, prizes, and stimulating lessons. But most of all, they responded well to positive, respectful treatment, much of which they had never had much of.

Well again I pulled together my ever-growing experiences as an educator to find my way with yet another crop of new students, new colleagues and new bosses. The challenge continues. I seem to go on and on having more fun and pleasure the further I go.

On August 6, 2004, I officially retired from the NYC Public School System after over 32 years. And guess what? I am about to begin my "second career" out here in my now home state of New Jersey. I have accepted a new position as a math teacher at Columbia HS in Maplewood NJ. I will be teaching, among other subjects, AP Calculus. And I just completed a one week training session on the techniques of teaching this most rigorous class. As always, teachers must "keep current" as to the latest strategies of the given subject at hand.

Good luck to all of you. I hope you all have as wonderful, exciting and challenging a career in education as I've had—and continue to have!! Always remain positive and optimistic about the possibilities. They are truly endless!!

FIGURE 17: STORIES TO GO WITH THE OLYMPIC LESSONS FROM FIGURES 6 AND 11

THE BATTLE OF THE BRIANS

The 1988 Winter Olympics, also known as the Calgary (Canada) Games, was one of the most exciting and dramatic in history. There were many outstanding contests and thrilling and poignant stories behind a great percentage of them. One of the most dramatic ones was, as the media dubbed it, "The Battle of the Brians." It was for men's figure skating gold, and it featured Brian Orser, the Canadian hometown favorite, versus Brian Boitano of the USA.

The preliminary competition had involved the "school figures," wherein Orser finished a close third to the second place Boitano. However, the next day, Orser recaptured the lead with a stunning performance in the short "free-skating" program. The gold was now Orser's to win or lose. This set up the showdown for that final long free-skating evening. In the final free-skating competition, Boitano wound up skating first, his favorite spot in the order. Some love to lead off the roster of competitors and others relish performing last. Years of practice were behind him now.

Olympic figure skating, of course, takes very hard work, extreme sacrifice, and faith in yourself and in your support staff. Skaters are always working to eliminate any Achilles heel that might exist. One's emotions must be well-harnessed to succeed. Skaters do become close, and there does arise a common bond of good feeling, mutual support and love as a result of all the emotional energy invested and the camaraderie formed.

In the final, Brian Boitano skated the performance of a lifetime—he hit all the jumps beautifully and flawlessly. In addition, he skated with uncharacteristic emotion. Some said it was the best free-skate performance ever! When it was over, it was over for Boitano. It was enormously gratifying. His eyes focused on the heavens above. Brian Boitano had sought to give the best performance he could...and that is what he did! If he lost, so be it; he could not control this. He did not even bother to view his competitors. He was at peace with himself. He had won his "inner" Olympics. This was success for Mr. Boitano.

Orser was up two skaters later, and he just was not at his best. Perhaps it was exhaustion; perhaps it was all the pressure. Who knows? Boitano would be the gold medalist. Orser came for tangible gold, not "inner" gold, and, as a result, he was quite disappointed.

Previous to this final, the pressure during the "build-up" was truly enormous. The dynamic duo handled the stress in differing ways however. Orser surrounded himself with a huge support network at most times. He had coaches, psychologists, dieticians and others to keep him company. Boitano only had his main two coaches with him. Orser had in the past had a reputation for "choking" under pressure, although he recently defeated Boitano in the '87 World Championships. Orser really was quite hungry for Olympic gold. Boitano was usually very talkative, but in the week before the finals, he became quite withdrawn. He needed to channel his emotions into the task at hand. Orser did work with his psychologist and also listened to relaxation tapes.

Boitano's incredibly soulful performance just turned out to be too overwhelming for Orser. The Battle of the Brians was truly as magnificent as it was expected to be.

EVENTS IN THE LIFE OF OLYMPIAN DAN JANSEN

It was in those '88 Winter Games at Calgary. The site was the speed-skating oval where Dan Jansen of Team USA was favored in the 500-meter sprint. He was the reigning World Champ in this event, and the day of the race was finally at hand. Only one problem, one major problem: Dan's sister Jane was dying from leukemia; in fact, her death was imminent. There had been a period when Jane's cancer went into remission, but it did not last. Gradually her health again began to unravel. At times in these situations, death can be considered, by some, a "godsend."

Dan spoke on the phone to Jane for the last time just half a day from the time his event was to begin. He knew that she would want him to race and not come home to be with her. Dan had been ready to donate bone marrow to his sister, but he was not an appropriate match. Had he done so, he probably wouldn't have been able to compete in the Games, for he would have been physically unable. Dan felt that he would trade in any gold medal for the healthy recovery of Jane. Unfortunately, this was not to be the case. Less than three hours after that final conversation, Dan got word that Jane had passed away. Dan's spirits were temporarily buoyed when he heard that the skating team dedicated the Games to his sister.

At 5 p.m., the race was about to begin. Jansen, though, felt different, lacking his usual pep and energy. Can we wonder why? Then, after a very uncharacteristic false start (one more and he would be disqualified), the race began. Only 13 seconds into the race, disaster struck. Dan Jansen (not so unaccountably) fell, and down with him went his hopes for any medal at all. In fact, the following week, he <u>again</u> fell in the 1,000.

Dan had nothing to be ashamed of. His beloved sister, Jane, had last seen him at one of his greatest victories—the '87 World Championships, where he stood on a pedestal higher up than anyone in the entire arena, and quite high in the eyes of his big sister as well!

Just why did Dan fall? How could it have happened, not once, but twice? Most psychologists would agree that the tragic events that Dan had to deal with were definitely factors in his "failure" at the Olympics. Fortunately, Dan did receive enormous support from his fiancée, Natalie, as well as from all of his eight brothers and sisters. This group was truly a pillar of support for the devastated Olympian.

It is often situations like these that permit us to philosophize about the importance of feelings and relationships over such material items as gold medals. Unfortunately, many of us must deal with family tragedies from time to time. This family illustrated the great need for strong support networks in our lives.

About the Author

Mark Richman is a veteran of 25 camp seasons in an assortment of roles–camper, counselor, group leader, Athletic Director and "King Of Mishigos." He had taught in the NYC public schools for 32 years—in middle school, in high school, and as an assistant principal at Erasmus HS in Brooklyn. He was the math staff and curriculum development specialist for the NYC Brooklyn and Staten Island high schools. In 2001, as Assistant Principal at The HS of Economics and Finance, a NYC HS across the street from "Ground Zero," he spent an amazing year that started on 9/11 and ended successfully in June. He helped his students escape injury on that fateful day as the co–leader of the closest school to the World Trade Center. He used his camp experiences to help lead his school through an evacuation and relocation that was the challenge of his career! He was a finalist in "The funniest teacher in NYC" contest and he has lectured nationally on issues related to camping and education. He is the author of 5 books on education, including "The Ultimate Camp Counselor Manual"–How To Succeed Magnificently At Summer Camp–Volume One. He is about to begin the third season of the next phase of his illustrious career as he took the role of math teacher at Columbia HS in Maplewood, N.J.

Rachel Richman is the daughter of Mark Richman. She is 12 years old (here in 2006) and is attending Millburn Middle School. Like her dad, she has enjoyed summer camp for many years and has contributed numerous insights into this second edition. In summer of 2005 and 2006, she had an amazing experience at Camp Ramah in the Berkshires. Some of her thoughts and reflections are incorporated into this book–especially in Chapter One—to give a camper's point of view as well. She contributed much to the spirit inherent in this book. She attended the South Mountain School in Millburn New Jersey before graduating in June of 2005. Her favorite activities at camp are soccer, swimming and spending time with friends.

978-0-595-40832-0
0-595-40832-X

Made in the USA
Lexington, KY
02 March 2015